RUNNING
with
Turtles

RUNNING
with *Turtles*

Bill Wilson

METRO
WORLD CHILD

New York, New York

Copyright © 2014 by Bill Wilson
Running with Turtles

ISBN 978-0-615-94316-9

Printed in the United States of America

Published by Metro World Child
PO Box 409
Brooklyn, NY 11237

Web site: www.metroworldchild.org

Contents

Introduction

If you see a turtle sitting on a fencepost, you can bet he didn't get there by himself!

—Alex Haley (1921-1992)[1]

Turtles belong on the ground or in the water. That is their natural habitat. A turtle on a fence post is quite an unusual sight and elicits the question, "How did it get there?" In an interview with the renowned author of the blockbuster book and movie, *Roots*, Anne Crowley reports seeing a picture in Alex Haley's home of a turtle positioned on top of a fence post. When asked about the picture Haley responded, *"Anytime you see a turtle on top of a fence post, you know he had some help."*

Most Christians that I've met in the past fifty years of full-time ministry move so slow that they can't get out of their own way. They've been stuck on one speed because of the church they grew up in, the denomination they're a part of, habits they've formed over the years— all things that keep them from making a difference. Don't get me wrong, they want to make a difference, but in order for that to happen, something has to change. If you're going to choose to run with turtles, your options are limited.

I've had to learn to run with people in this turtle adventure. In doing so, I've found that either I have to slow down to their pace or get out in front of them and encourage them to pick up their own pace. Water boils at 212 degrees Fahrenheit, or 100 degrees Celsius depending on what part of the world you're reading this in. It does not boil at 210 or 211; but at 212 degrees there is a moment when the heat forces the water to change. At that exact moment, it becomes unrecognizable from what it was moments before. My prayer is that this book will bring about that moment in your life—a defining moment when you will no longer be what you once were, but you will become unrecognizable to those around you.

This book is the story of the many characters in the Bible who were placed on a fence post and demonstrated that they belonged there, above those other turtles that walked below them. Their prominence was made possible by their commitment to a higher purpose that was motivated by a higher law—the law of love.

Running with Turtles is for men and women who face the challenges that life brings them and discover victory in the midst of conflict. On the anvil of conflict and controversy our lives can be forged into a mighty weapon for the purposes of God. The Lord has helped me, and through this book, I believe it will help some turtles get faster and stand out amongst others.

Chapter 1

The Power of Influence: You Are a Cedar to Somebody

Every soul that touches yours
be it the slightest contact
gets there from some good
some little grace, one kindly thought;
one inspiration yet unfelt.[1]

owl, fir tree; for the cedar is fallen; because the mighty are spoiled: howl, O ye oaks of Bashan; for the forest of the vintage is come down (Zechariah 11:2).

At a quick glance I can imagine you are thinking, "What does this verse have to do with anything?" I have always loved the Old Testament, and I see things that I don't believe others see. In this verse is a powerful truth, hidden from the eyes of the ordinary reader. In a nutshell, here is the truth in this verse: You are a cedar to somebody.

The Hebrew language is more metaphoric, while the Greek language is more didactic. The writers of the Old Testament drew pictures with their words and there was always a hidden meaning behind those pictures. Many of the words had prophetic meaning attached to them. The writers of the Old Testament often used trees as metaphors for kings and kingdoms. Over the years I have studied and preached a lot on this subject. Some of the titles of those messages go like this: "When the Axe is Laid to the Root of the Tree," "Whose Branches Run Over the Wall," and "Leave the Fruit Trees Alone."

When you consider trees, branches, fruit, leaves, stumps, and roots, they're always used as a metaphor and a type of something that can be applied in our lives. There are many kinds of trees mentioned in the Bible, such as the fig tree, olive tree, acacia, sycamore, terabinth, almond, oak, cedar, fir and others. All of these trees have symbolic meaning.

> Whether you like it or not, your life has influence on others.

In this verse, three specific trees are mentioned: fir, cedar and oak. The great trees in the forest, like the cedar and the oak, have a profound influence on the lesser, smaller trees that they dwarf. They provide covering and protection. In the context of this verse, these trees have huge prophetic meaning. The prophetic message is clear. Whether you like it or not, your life has influence on others. You do not live in a vacuum. Your life touches others and the more exposure you have on others, the greater the influence, for good or for evil. One of the keys to leadership is influence. It is even greater than authority. Your position in life determines the degree of that influence.

Cedars of Lebanon

I am sure that you have heard the term, *Cedars of Lebanon.* They are mentioned throughout the Old Testament with great admiration. Wherever these great trees grew, they were considered to be the glory of Lebanon, where these great cedar trees grew. They were described as majestic, powerful and excellent. In Ezekiel 31:3-5 the Assyrian power is compared to:

> *...a cedar in Lebanon with fair branches, and with a shadowing shroud, and of an high stature; and his top was among the thick boughs. The waters made him great, the deep set him up on high with her rivers running round about his plants, and sent her little rivers unto all the trees of the field. Therefore his height was exalted above all the trees of the field, and his boughs were multiplied, and his branches became long because of the multitude of waters, when he shot forth.*

The wood of the cedar has always been highly prized. David had a house of cedar built for him by Hiram, king of Tyre (2 Samuel 5:11). Cedar timber was very much used in the construction of Solomon's temple and palace. These trees were cut down in Lebanon by Sidonians under orders of the King of Tyre (1 Kings 5:6-10).

"As young trees, cedars are cone-shaped, but as they age, the branches spread and flatten. Cedars of Lebanon grow up to 90 feet tall and may live 3000 years."[2] The wood of the cedar trees was a popular building commodity that was used for trusses, beams, ceilings, pillars and foundations. One last valuable thing about the cedar tree is that its resin preserves it from rot and insects.

The Mighty Oak

The oak trees were well-known in biblical times for their majestic height and massive trunks. Because of this they were a symbol of power and pride as indicated in Isaiah 2:12-13. *For the day of the LORD of hosts shall be upon every one that is proud and lofty, and upon every one that is lifted up; and he shall be brought low: And upon all the cedars of Lebanon, that are high and lifted up, and upon all the oaks of Bashan…*

The wood from the oak trees of Bashan were used to make the oars that were used to power their ships.

The oak tree was often used as a place of rest and retreat as seen in 1 Kings 13:14, *And went after the man of God, and found him sitting under an oak: and he said unto him, Art thou the man of God that camest from Judah? And he said, I am.*

In 1 Chronicles 10:12 we discover that the mighty oak was used as a burial ground: *They arose, all the valiant men, and took away the body of Saul, and the bodies of his sons, and brought them to Jabesh, and buried their bones under the oak in Jabesh, and fasted seven days.*

Joshua took the book of the law and planted it under a mighty oak as seen in Joshua 24:26. *And Joshua wrote these words in the book of the law of God, and took a great stone, and set it up there under an oak, that was by the sanctuary of the LORD.*

Finally, as seen in the words of Ezekiel 6:13, the oak was often chosen as a place of great idolatry. *Then shall ye know that I am the LORD, when their slain men shall be among their idols round about their altars, upon every high hill, in all the tops of the mountains, and under every green tree, and under every thick oak, the place where they did offer sweet savour to all their idols.*

The Humble Fir

Now, we reach the final tree in this study: the fir tree, sometimes known as the pine fir. The fir tree was much more humble than the glorious cedar and the mighty oak. It wasn't small or flimsy, but lesser in stature and use than the other two. The fir tree was straight and plain and had the same protective resin as the cedar. It was used to make furniture and musical instruments in Old Testament times. *And David and all the house of Israel played before the LORD on all manner of instruments made of fir wood, even on harps, and on psalteries, and on timbrels, and on cornets, and on cymbals* (2 Samuel 6:5).

It is covered with a fruit, better known to us as a pine cone, and becomes an edible nut as indicated in Hosea 14:8: *Ephraim shall say, What have I to do any more with idols? I have heard him, and observed him: I am like a green fir tree. From me is thy fruit found.*

The fir tree has been referred to in the book of Isaiah as a sign of restoration and deliverance. *Instead of the thorn shall come up the fir tree, and instead of the brier shall come up the myrtle tree: and is shall be to the LORD for a name, for an everlasting sign that shall not be cut off* (Isaiah 55:13).

Under a Covering or a Crushing

So, you have these forests where the cedars of Lebanon and the powerful oak trees grow. Right next to them, growing in the exact same forest, are the little fir trees. There they are, side by side, growing together on Mount Herman.

Consider this picture. The small fir tree lives under the protective covering of the mightier trees in the forest. When a great storm slams into the forest, the cedar and the oak are impacted by the power of the wind and rain because they stick up higher and are more exposed to the storm. The small tree experiences none of the excitement and drama of the storm and no one notices. If the fir tree falls, who will notice? But if the cedar falls, or if the oak falls, the effect of that fall is horrific for the smaller trees that are impacted. With one great crash it could crush and destroy many of the smaller trees. These great trees can be a covering or a crushing. They can protect or they can pulverize. They can shield or squash.

> A spiritual cedar is a person who has withstood the tests of time, who has grown strong and matured and has huge influence over the lives of those who follow them, listen to them and are exposed to them.

Because of its closeness to the cedar or oak, the fir comes under a powerful influence of these trees, for good or for bad. As it is for the trees of the forest, so it is in the life of mankind. We either influence others or we are influenced by others.

A spiritual cedar is a person who has withstood the tests of time, who has grown strong and matured and has huge influence over the lives of those who follow them, listen to them and are exposed to them. They have great influence over the young lives around them. The way they live their lives can either cover and protect or crush and pound.

Before I move on, I want to make one thing clear. It is my personal rule on how I respond to the fall of a leader, whether they are a pastor or a television personality. Here it is: I have nothing to say. I choose to not be drawn into the gossip and blather of others who want to chatter on about the fall of a leader. I reject the superficial spirituality of those who seek to know more, so they can pray.

Number one, we don't necessarily know all that is going on, and secondly, it is not our business. People love to gossip under the guise of a phony position. It has nothing to do with anybody wanting to pray for someone. People just like to talk. They like to gossip. They like to tear people down. It is unfortunate, but it is true. Eleanor Roosevelt said that "great minds discuss ideas. Average minds discuss events. Small minds discuss people."[3] Someone else said that gossip is the opiate of the masses. There is a certain inclination to want to engage in "juicy" stuff. But that fondness for rumors must be tamed and conquered.

> Leaders need to be careful because the higher they go, the greater the danger.

Better to pray and shut your mouth. That's why most people do not approach me on this kind of thing because they know I just refuse to take the bait. I don't get drawn into the gossip, into the foolishness, and into "what do you think?"

Number two, leaders need to be careful because the higher they go, the greater the danger. As someone has said, "New levels, new devils." There is the temptation to think that we are a little bit better, a little bit smarter, and a little bit stronger than those around us. Pride comes before a fall. When our eyes shift from how great God is to how great we are there will be trouble.

What's YOUR Kryptonite?

Kryptonite is a meteor-like substance that was found on Superman's home planet, Krypton. Whenever Superman was exposed to that glowing green substance, he was weakened and left helpless. His enemies used Kryptonite to debilitate him and bring him down. Now, let me state this: all of us deal with stuff, and you had better know what your kryptonite is. What are the weak and vulnerable areas of your life?

Everybody has a kryptonite. Everybody, I don't care who you are. Everybody has it. I have it, and you have it. I have dealt with anger all my life. I still deal with it. I have no problem talking about it. I'll probably deal with it all my life, but you know what? I'm smart enough to know it. So, do you know what I have to do? I have to make sure I don't allow myself to get put into a position where my anger gets the best of me. I don't have any problem telling you this because all of us need to realize we have something that we deal with. If you don't know what your kryptonite is, you might just fall prey to its power. If you ignore it, it will bite you.

The apostle Paul talked about his thorn in the flesh—his kryptonite—describing it as a weakness that helped keep him from rising to the place of spiritual pride. He begged God to take it away. Finally, God responded to Paul's prayer with these words: *And He said to me, My grace is sufficient for thee: for My strength is made perfect in weakness* (2 Corinthians 12:9). Kryptonite can only be conquered by the power of grace, the place where our weakness is transformed into strength.

Too many people think that they are invincible and it is only when they fall that they discover their own personal kryptonite. Your kryptonite is going to be different than mine. Human kryptonite comes in many different forms: anger, lust, fear, insecurity and many other forms. You may be dealing with a myriad of kryptonite. Dealing with it begins with acknowledging it. Once you see it then you must protect yourself from people or situations that will cause you to fall. Don't let dirty thoughts or people with dirty feet get into your head.

I have my kryptonite. You've got yours. We all need to be working on it every day. I do. I have learned that when exposed to my kryptonite,

I must be cautious. I need insight into the nature of the kryptonite and exercise discernment when confronted with a situation that might weaken me. A good example is about the guy that walks down the same road five times and falls in the same hole. No matter what he does, he never sees the hole and always falls in. What would your advice be to that guy? Go down a different road.

> Before you can heal others, you must be healed.

It is as simple as that. Avoid those places and/or people that expose you to your own kryptonite.

You need to take care of your own self because you are a cedar to somebody. If you take care of yourself, you won't hurt others. Before you can heal others, you must be healed. You won't find this in most leadership books, but it is an important principle. What you do and who you are has tremendous impact on others. Best to find your kryptonite before it hurts you and someone else.

You Are a Cedar to Somebody

You're a cedar to somebody. Somebody grows beneath your branches. You need to get this. This is a truth that must be thoroughly understood by all of those in places of power and influence. I don't always like being responsible. Does that surprise you? I am responsible for so much, that if anyone gives me one more thing to be responsible for, I'm going to explode. I do not need one more responsibility in my life. But that's what I signed up for. If you want to be in the ministry, or any leadership position, don't complain when you have to work hard and be responsible for others. If you want to be in leadership, don't complain when you have to put in more hours. Don't complain when you are misunderstood. This is what you signed up for. If you don't want to be in a place of influence, go sell cars or work at a fast food restaurant.

It's something like getting a driver's license. When you are old enough, you have the right to get a driver's license. However, with that right come responsibilities. You have to obey the laws of the road. You have to drive defensively. You have to be careful and vigilant. Every right is accompanied with a responsibility.

Being a cedar to others requires much. How you approach that responsibility is critical. To be effective you have to keep God in His rightful place. Is He the steering wheel or is He a spare tire? He's one or the other. Either He steers you, directs you, guides you, OR you take the steering wheel and become the master controller. If you are going to be a positive influence on others, you need to live under His control. You are a cedar to somebody. Somebody is under your influence. Example is not the main thing in influencing others—it is the *only* thing.

If The Cedar Falls, Many Will Fall

The fir tree is not as influential as the cedar. If one of the kids in our Sunday school falls, it will not affect the teacher and it will not be as impactful as the teacher falling. The fewer the number of people in your life and degree of influence determines the extent that your possible failure will have on others. The greater the influence, the greater the damage it will have.

If you are in a place of leadership, your fall will impact many. I have worked with hundreds of people over the years, and I am extremely cautious about who I put in a place of influence in our ministry. I am not looking for names or degrees. I am looking for faithfulness, tested character, and proven worth. I cannot entrust the lives of these kids into the hands of a novice who is more interested in position than service, the pulpit rather than the street. Who you are is just as important as what you do. I look for people who understand these truths.

When you move into places of responsibility and influence you become a cedar to somebody. Ask yourself right now, who are you a cedar to this day? Who is looking at you today? Who is watching you today? Who is depending on you today? Who is looking forward to seeing

> Who is watching you today? Who is depending on you today? Who is looking forward to seeing you today?

you today? Who is waiting for you to arrive today? Who is going to be waiting for you to arrive tomorrow? Who is depending on you to preach? Who's depending on you to lead? Because you are a cedar to somebody, if you fail, it will have a negative effect on others.

Athletes in the world of sports are role models whether they like it or not. If they should fall, it can be devastating to those young kids who love and follow them. In some ways we are all role models—people of influence—but the greater your influence and following, the greater for good or for evil. Just like the mighty oak tree, the greater your sphere of influence, the greater damage you can do if you fall.

When Mexican politician and general Santa Ana (1794-1876) was meeting with his men the night before they went into the Battle of the Alamo, the pivotal event in the Texas Revolution, he told them that when they got inside the walls of the Alamo that they were to shoot the men with the brass buttons on their uniforms. What did that mean? Take out their leaders. Aim for them. Take them out. By the way, that's exactly what the devil does, because he's smart enough to know that if you can take out the leader, you can bring down the house.

The beauty of Israel is slain upon thy high places: how are the mighty fallen! (2 Samuel 1:19). Saul and Jonathan had just fallen at the hands of the enemy, and David lamented the demise of these great leaders in Israel. No one is too great that they cannot experience the shambles of Saul. Their fall not only destroys their fortunes, but it destroys the fortunes of others. When a leader or a government fails, everyone under them is adversely affected.

> You might be able to dodge your responsibilities, but you will never be able to dodge the consequences of avoiding your responsibilities.

Both the cedar and the fir tree were used in the house of God. Both were needed. The difference is in the place they are used. If the ceiling, made of fir, should crash, it is not as devastating as if the cedar foundation should collapse. Both are important, but one has greater consequence than the other. The higher you climb the leadership ladder, the greater the impact on those beneath you.

The Price of Greatness is Responsibility

One of the major truths of this book is that the higher up the ladder you go, the more your underwear shows. In other words, the higher you go, the greater your exposure. The greater the exposure you have, the greater your responsibility. The willingness to accept responsibility for your life and the lives of others is a sign of great character. Once you have become responsible for someone, you are being moved to another level. You have just become a cedar to somebody, and your responsibility has increased. In the future, you might be able to dodge your responsibilities, but you will never be able to dodge the consequences of avoiding your responsibilities.

Are leaders perfect? Well, I haven't found a perfect leader, and I doubt that you have. As we have already stated, we all have our kryptonite. The difference is that great leaders have learned how to live responsibly and in the awareness of those weaknesses. They live in the constant awareness that they are shaping the lives of others and must be careful about what enters their thinking and what influences their actions. When you are in a position of leadership or influence, there are eyes watching you everywhere you go. If you cannot accept that and if you feel that the burden is too great, then leadership is not for you.

Whether you like it or not, responsible leadership will affect your privacy. I'm not saying that this is either right or wrong. I'm not saying it's easy. I'm not saying that I even like it. I remember one time that I had made one of my many trips to Tulsa. I had just landed at the airport and all I wanted to do was go to the Rib Crib, my favorite restaurant in Tulsa. The timing was perfect. I would avoid the rush. All I wanted to do was relax in peace as I dove into the food. It was a very busy time of the year, traveling and trying to get everything ready for our Christmas season. I was tired and hungry and just wanted to get to the Rib Crib that was just down the street from Oral Roberts University. We got to the restaurant, and I ordered my little chicken sandwich, beans and their delicious coleslaw.

I'm very predictable. I could eat the same thing every day. Just as I was ready to dive into the food, I heard someone with a shrill voice yell my name. I can't say what I was thinking. All I wanted to do was eat my little sandwich, eat my beans, and be left alone. I guess it was inevitable. I have preached in that town so many times. But, I just wanted to eat without drama. In the midst of those irritating feelings, I thought to myself, *What do you expect? You're on television all over the world. You are doing this because you have to raise the money for the ministry. Everything hinges on you sharing the vision and motivating people to stand with you. And now you're mad because they won't let you eat your beans in peace?* All of a sudden, I just started laughing at the absurdity of it all. The more I thought about it, the harder I laughed. What else could I do? Others see when you lead! There is no escaping it. Therefore, you must accept it.

Finding Your Level

One thing that I have always tried to communicate to others is the need to constantly be who you are. Whether I am preaching on a platform or eating at the Rib Crib, I always seek to be consistent with the person that I am. That's why I don't put on a show on the platform like many television preachers do. Too much of it is for show. I can't do that. I won't do that. I am what I am. I won't pretend to be something that I am not. I don't go into a "preaching mode." Please understand me. I have found a level of life that I can live. I know what it takes to do what I do, and I have found a level in life that I am content with. I feel comfortable in my own skin and don't need to act like others. I don't try to do more or less than I can. And I would challenge you to do the same.

We will never find our level until we are willing to go beyond where we have ever gone. Don't seek more, but don't settle for less. I have watched some folks come to our ministry and stay here for many years. They have faithfully served. They have sacrificed much. They found their level. Others could not make it for a month. They didn't find a level. Some of them have never found it.

I couldn't imagine myself living in any other place. New York City is my home. I am comfortable here. I am not a small town guy. You might be different. The city might not be for you. You have to find your own level, your own place, your own ministry that is divinely designed for you. Wherever you are, you will find your level if you don't give up. Your place becomes the space where you are trained, equipped, and released. You have to discover what you can do and what you cannot do, what you can and cannot endure. Many could not do what I do: the constant travel, the long days and nights, the burden I bear for others, the stress of raising enough money to support our vision and much, much more. I had to find my own level of what I can handle. You have to find yours for yourself.

Whatever your level is, it will require denying yourself, putting others first, making the sacrifice, enduring indifference and misunderstanding, surviving the storms and remaining faithful in all you do.

I remember the day when I got the report that my home pastor had committed suicide. In the report they recorded that after they broke down the door, they said it looked like he was trying to reach for the telephone. I don't know what that means. I've tried not to read too much into it. Here is the truth. This man, who had influenced my life so much, had fallen. You are a cedar to somebody, aren't you? Wherever you go, somebody is looking at you. The very small things you do impacts others. A simple hug, a passing pat on the back, a listening ear or some other sign of caring! Conversely, a negative act can influence people. An ignoring look, an uncaring act, or a dreadful fall! I don't know who's watching you today. I'm not even sure I know who's watching me, but my prayer is that you will realize that you have influence and you have impact on the lives of others. I pray that you will always live in the awareness of that great truth.

Chapter 2

Stand for Something:
Everybody Left But One

*Give us clear vision that we may know where to
stand and what to stand for—because unless we
stand for something we shall fall for anything.*[1]

I f there was a Mount Rushmore of the great leaders of the Bible,
the Apostle Paul's image would certainly be one of the more promi-
nent faces engraved into that mountain. The transition from Saul the
persecutor to Paul the apostle was a journey peppered with pain and
salted with success. His conversion became one of the more important
chapters in the history of the Church. More than any other character in
the New Testament, Paul was responsible for the spread of the Gospel
and the establishment of the Church throughout the Roman Empire.

For the first time, we meet his spiritual son, Timothy, in Acts 16. At
the beginning of his second missionary journey, Paul arrived in Lystra

and Derbe. While in that area, he was introduced to Timothy, whose father was a Greek and mother was a Jew. Timothy had been greatly influenced by the faith of his mother and grandmother. He came to the faith at an early age and was eager to serve God. In the meeting with Paul, a friendship was formed, one that would last for a lifetime. Paul made the decision, one that was received with great joy, that Timothy would join this missionary band. Throughout his life, Paul was clear in his intentions toward Timothy. He found in Timothy a young man who could carry the dreams of Paul into the next generation.

Paul had reached the end of his life and was now ready to pen his final words to his beloved son. We read those words in the two letters he wrote to Timothy. The letters are Paul's final instructions to his faithful friend.

After Paul's first release from prison in Rome, he wrote his first letter to Timothy and another to Titus. After those letters he was imprisoned again under the reign of Nero. It was during this timeframe that he crafted his second letter to Timothy. His second incarceration was much different than the first. He was not under house arrest, as in his first stay in prison. This time he was thrown into a cold dungeon and chained like a common criminal. His friends had forsaken him. Most everyone in Asia, including Demas, had abandoned him. Only Luke remained with him. Paul was eager for Timothy to join him, but I suspect that he knew that he would die before Timothy could make the trip. Timothy, without a doubt, was his favorite son. He had been faithful to him and loved him deeply. In Philippians 2:20 Paul declared that he had no one else like Timothy.

> Before the training/ equipping process can begin there must be a respect of the student for the teacher.

Respect for the Teacher

A lot of sermons and books have been written about discipleship. In these days, one of the most commonly used buzz words is *mentoring*. Whether you want to call it discipleship or mentoring, one thing is true. You cannot disciple/mentor one who does not respect you. Before the training/equipping process can begin there must be a respect of the student for the teacher. That respect cannot be forced, manipulated or contrived. It can only be attained through a natural process. It is the mentor's life and words that command that respect. Mentoring in and of itself will not work. Without respect, you will not be open to receive direction, instruction or reproof from someone no matter how good the advice is, no matter how good the mentoring is, and no matter how much sense someone's advice will make. That's why it's very important to be careful who is speaking into your life. You have to be very, very careful who you take advice from. I've watched many people take advice from folks they shouldn't have, spending time around people, even in the ministry, that they should have avoided. Why? Because it's not just about mentoring! It's not just about someone giving advice. Information is not enough, especially if it's coming from someone for whom it has not worked. There are a lot of people out there selling books, giving information, doing seminars, but at the end of the day, you need to ask yourself, "Has their knowledge been proven in their life?" Does their life market their message?

When David rejected Saul's weapons he did so, not because he had not proved them, but because he really didn't respect Saul. I would find it nearly impossible to take something—help—from someone that I didn't respect. If someone gives you a weapon to use, you had better have respect for the weapon and you need to respect the one who's giving it. Respect is not given, it is earned.

Back to the relationship between Paul and Timothy, we see a bond built upon respect. Timothy would have no problem receiving input in his life from Paul because Paul was a proven warrior. His life was consistent with his words.

I approach mentoring today differently than I did twenty years ago because I am not the same person I was then. I look at things differently. I am not impressed with great sermons that are dramatically presented. I look at the person behind the words. Philosophies and priorities change over the years as we grow and mature. Things that were important to us when we were young do change. The depth of our message and the breadth of our experiences grow through the trials and hardships we walk through. Knowledge and education can make you smart, but not mature. Mature leaders draw from the content gained from their experiences and personal revelations, not from the content of a book.

The Urgency of the Moment

This was a critical time in Paul's life. He was in a prison cell and he knew that his life was about to come to an end. There was urgency in the moment. Looking backward, he reflected on the price he had paid to further the message of Christ and to build His Church: stoned, beaten, imprisoned, abandoned for dead, shipwrecked, betrayed, ostracized, criticized, and rejected.

The acclaimed poet, Robert Browning, penned a poignant poem, entitled, *A Death in the Desert*. The poem is a fictional piece that reflects the final thoughts of the Apostle John. One of the verses, I am sure, reflected a thought that would be similar to Paul's thinking at this final stage of his life. The thought centers on the question of what would happen to the Church when there were none left whose eyes had seen the Lord and felt the power of His words. The question haunted him. What would happen when no one was alive who knew Him?

> *"If I live yet, it is for good, more love*
>   *'Through me to men: be nought but ashes here*
>   *"That keep awhile my semblance, who was John,—*
>   *"Still, when they scatter, there is left on earth*
>   *"No one alive who knew (consider this!)*
>   *"—Saw with his eyes and handled with his hands*
>   *"That which was from the first, the Word of Life.*
>   *"How will it be when none more saith 'I saw'"?* [2]

Though there were those who rejected him. There were those who respected and loved him. But, here is the truth of this matter. He was more admired after his death than during his life. I have often said, "You will always be more popular in death." When you die, they name parks after you. They name streets after you.

> Depending on the number of people you have influenced, your funeral will be better attended than your birthday party.

They write about you in textbooks. Depending on the number of people you have influenced, your funeral will be better attended than your birthday party. After I was shot in New York, I received emails from people I had not heard from for twenty years.

In his letter to Timothy, Paul was trying to set things in order before his departure. He had invested much into Timothy's life and knew that he would become a successor to Paul. In his mind, he was constrained by the thoughts of a future without him and pressed in to write what would be his final words to his spiritual son. Facing death's door, he was still teaching and exhorting Timothy. He knew that the time of his departure was at hand. He had fought the fight. He had finished his course. Now, this was the time for Timothy to take the baton and carry the battle into the next generation.

Everyone Left But One

*For Demas hath forsaken me, having loved this present world, and is departed unto Thessalonica; Crescens to Galatia, Titus unto Dalmatia. Only Luke is with me. Take Mark, and bring him with thee: for he is profitable to me for the ministry. And Tychicus have I sent to Ephesus. The cloke that I left at Troas with Carpus, when thou comest, bring with thee, and the books, but especially the parchments. Alexander the coppersmith did me much evil: the Lord reward him according to his works: Of whom be thou ware also; for he hath greatly withstood our words. At my first answer **no man stood with me, but all men forsook me**: I pray God that it may not be laid to their charge. **Notwithstanding the Lord stood with me**, and strengthened me; that by me the preaching might be fully known, and that all the Gentiles might hear: and I was delivered out of the mouth of the lion. And the Lord shall deliver me from every evil work, and will preserve me unto his heavenly kingdom: to whom be glory forever and ever. Amen.*

—2 Timothy 4:10-18 emphasis added

At some point, every person's hour will come. Much of the final days of a person's life are spent in reflection and setting his life in order. After he had given his final words of counsel to Timothy, he was ready to pen the final words. Even up to his final days, Paul suffered rejection and abuse. Demas had forsaken him. Alexander, a coppersmith, did him evil. He was forced to live with this personal pain till his dying days.

And they all left, but one! Everybody left, except one. Paul, the great apostle of the faith, was alone in a jail cell. Except for Luke, there was no one to take care of him. All his life he had taken care of others, and in his hour of need, where were his helpers? I know that feeling. Over the years many people have told me that if I need them, all I had to do was call and they would be there. To be truthful, very few have answered that call. I am thankful for those few, but it makes you wonder. When your back is against the wall, when you really need somebody, as we say, to stand with you, they're hard to find, aren't they? You discover your true friends in times of adversity. I am reminded of the words

> Sometimes God is the only one who stands with you.

of that great American soldier, Ulysses S. Grant (1822-1885), when he said, "The friend in my adversity I shall always cherish most. I can better trust those who helped to relieve the gloom of my dark hours than those who are so ready to enjoy with me the sunshine of my prosperity."[3] How very true his words are! It is as someone once said, "In prosperity our friends know us; in adversity we know our friends."

I can imagine Paul thinking this way. "When my hour came, I would have thought somebody would have been there for me. What about all the people that were healed through my ministry? What about the ministries I helped to launch? What about all the people that met Christ through my words? Surely, there would have been more people here with me at this time." In spite of this great sadness impinging upon his soul, Paul was learning once again that sometimes God is the only one who stands with you. Forever, God is your source and strength. He is the ever-faithful One.

Who is Your Source?

Before we move to the main thought of this chapter, I have to make one thing clear. It might be one of the most important lessons you learn in life. People are not your source! They are not your source for happiness. They are not your source for finances. They are not your source for strength. I am not saying that there will never be people in your life who bring you joy, financial support, or spiritual assistance. I am saying that people will never be the supreme source of your life. If you are looking to others to make you happy or rich, you will be disappointed. You are looking in the wrong direction. Ultimately, neither your happiness nor your success can come from other people. At some point, you will realize that God is the One who will stand with you. Once you discover that truth, you won't be looking at other people to fill the voids in your life.

I have to admit that I think differently than most people. While reading this I was thinking that now would be a good time for Paul to give Timothy a good dose of reality. Let him know what's really out there. "It isn't worth it. Nobody will appreciate you. Everybody is a fraud and a fake. Sure, they have nice words for you when they are with you, but then they will lie about you behind your back. Nobody will support you. They all have their own agendas. Timothy, you might as well avoid the pain and suffering and find another job." He was dying. It was over. He had nothing to lose at this point. This would have been the time he could have written and said, "Go work at Sears. Go! Go now! Run! Get on a boat! Run for your life! Get out of here!"

> The encouraging words from the Lord are preserved for those in the place of affliction.

Obviously, that is not what he did. But he might have thought about it for a moment. What did he tell Timothy? "You can't count on folks, no matter what they say. People will leave you, but the Lord stood with me. He is my source, and He is my support."

The Lord Stood with Me

"Notwithstanding the Lord stood with me, and strengthened me." We will never know the reality of these words until we have lived in the ditch of a dilemma and wandered on an island of isolation. The comforting words of the Lord are reserved for those who have no comfort. The encouraging words from the Lord are preserved for those in the place of affliction. It is in those moments that His words become precious as gold.

In the Bible we see God taking different human characteristics. In theology, we call this an *anthropomorphic* term. *Anthropomorphic* means "the application of a human characteristic or attribute to God." We have read that the Lord *sits* on His throne, or that the Lord *walks* with a person or that the Lord *stands* at the door and knocks, or the Lord's *eyes move* to and fro throughout the earth. When these types of phrases are used in the Bible, they are used to explain, in human terms, the activity of God.

For instance, when we read that Jesus sat down at the right hand of the Father, it is implying a certain truth. When you sit down, you are taking a place of rest. A chair is a piece of furniture that was designed for resting. Furthermore, when Jesus sits at the right hand of the Father, it is also indicating a place of authority. Combining these truths, the Scripture is telling us that Jesus takes a place of rest. His work is done, completed. There is nothing else for Him to do, but rest from His labor. Also, it means that this place of rest is a place of authority.

"The Lord stood with me." This phrase reminds me of two different locations that amplify this truth. The first one is a board meeting. Everyone is seated in their chairs around the board room with the CEO seated at the head of the table. When he stands, it is a signal to all at the table that the meeting is over. There is nothing else to be said or done. Meeting adjourned! The second place is a courtroom. When a judge asks the defendant to stand, the attorney stands with him. When decisions are about to be made that will affect your life, someone is there standing with you. They have supported you and defended you throughout the process.

> In your greatest adversity, the Lord will stand with you.

So, Paul was telling Timothy that at the time of his greatest trial, the Lord was there standing with him, supporting and defending him. As you are reading this right now, I want you to know that in your greatest adversity, the Lord will stand with you. Though others abandon you, He will never leave you, nor forsake you. He positions Himself, on your behalf, as a prop and a proponent, a support and an advocate.

Those who have experienced both the mountaintop and the valley live in a different arena than other people. Their worship is not dependent on a great band and a dynamic worship leader. Their worship arises out of those deep places within that have been touched by God in the times of trials. They have experienced the goodness of the Lord. They have felt His presence when dark clouds have overshadowed their lives. David, the greatest psalmist ever, wrote his songs during some of the most difficult times of his life. In his prosperity he experienced times of fear and in his greatest affliction he enjoyed times of comfort. The Lord was his writer's muse, his inspiration. The Lord stood with him.

Once you've been through some things, once you've been through some battles, once you've been through some struggles, it doesn't matter if somebody sings well or not. That doesn't affect my praise. That doesn't affect my worship. I don't need to be inspired by others for I have been inspired by the Lord. I worship because the Lord stood with me. My catalyst for worship is the deep knowing in my spirit that God has been with me through it all.

We have something to thank God for. We all have something to be grateful for, don't we? You may have been through some hard stuff. You may have walked through dark places. You have been through some pain. But here you are. The Lord stood with you. See, that's when praise becomes personal, just like David's. Those who have been delivered from their afflictions and have been saved from their enemies, have a new song to sing:

> *He brought me up also out of an horrible pit, out of the miry clay, and set my feet upon a rock, and established my goings. And He hath put a new song in my mouth, even praise unto our God: many shall see it, and fear, and shall trust in the LORD.*
>
> —Psalm 40:2-3

You may have thought that your ministry was over. You may have thought that your marriage was over. You may have thought that your health was slipping away and death's door was staring you in the face. But the Lord stood with you. The Lord was there when others were not. He wiped away your tears. His grace made you bigger than you really were. He healed you. He saved you. He released you from your personal prison.

There's a bond that is built with someone who stands with you in a time of trouble. There is something wonderful and magical when someone standing next to you says, "I'm going to go through this with you no matter what it takes. I will stand with you no matter how deep the water gets. I'm going stand with you." Have you ever gone through something with somebody? It's hard to explain the sense of loyalty and commitment that you will, forever, have for them. It is a bond that cannot be broken. The Lord stood with Paul in his darkest moments and because God was faithful, Paul was faithful.

The Lord Stood For Me

The way the statement is made, it makes one think that they were both standing. *The Lord stood with me.* However, there will come a time in your life, Timothy, when you are not standing. You have been knocked out by the blows of your enemies, whether they are people or circumstances. When life gives you a punch in the gut, you lose your breath and fall to the ground. There is nothing like one of life's sucker punches when you least expect it. You go to the doctor for one of your regular checkups, not expecting anything, and then after the routine examination, he tells you that you have a lump and it is cancer.

> The Lord is there, and He will stand up for you when you cannot stand up for yourself.

Your boss calls you into his office for a conversation and you are told that the whole company has to be downsized and you are now let go. The unexpected moment can hit any of us at any time. There is no time to prepare or pray. Wham! A knockout punch has just landed and you find yourself helplessly on the canvas. What do you do? Where do you turn? At that point, the Lord will not only stand *with* you, but He'll stand *for* you.

The time will come when you cannot stand up for yourself and you need someone to help. The Lord is there, and He will stand up for you when you cannot stand up for yourself. It's one thing to stand in the midst of your battles and know that the Lord is standing alongside of you. But there comes another time when you just can't do it. You feel like you can't take it anymore. You have been beaten down and knocked out. You know you're supposed to take it. You know you ought to take it. There are people that expect you to take it. But you've just had it. You cannot take another disappointment. You cannot take any more bad news. You cannot take any more people walking out of your life. In those depressing, dark moments the Lord says, "I'll go for you. I'll stand up for you."

A while back I was thinking about the old days, when we first started buying property. I always went to the closings on new properties we were purchasing. I had to go. I had no one else I could depend upon. But now, I don't go to closings. I have an attorney that I trust and he goes for me. He can handle all of the legal matters for me. In fact, my attorney does not even want me to go. He knows that I don't need any more issues to deal with. It is just one burden that he can lift off my shoulders.

Here is another hidden truth in these words. There are times when you are trying to stand up for yourself, when you should allow the Lord stand up for you. You worry about stuff you shouldn't even be thinking about. You get all stressed out about things that are coming at you and the stress quickly turns to fear and extreme anxiety. There will come a time in your life when you learn how to cast all your burdens on the Lord. This is a critical lesson, learning how to let the Lord stand for you.

I remember when I was a kid, and we lived on the border of the Italian neighborhood of Boston. There was this group of five Italian kids that would pick on me every day. I was just a little runt and an easy target for them. I am not trying to disparage any Italians that are reading this book. I could be describing any people group anywhere in the world.

I would run to and from school every day just to avoid them. Finally, one day my sister heard about this bullying and was ready to put an end to it. She came to me and said, "I'll meet you at school today." And I said, "Okay." I didn't think much about it. Well, it was inevitable. These five thugs came up to me and my sister. It was freezing outside, and we all had our coats on. My sister had this big old kitchen knife that she had put in her coat. I had no clue what she was planning. So, these five guys came up, and she said, "You stay here. Let me deal with this." I said, "Okay." I took a couple of steps backward. She moved in on these guys and pulled out that knife. This is not an ordinary knife. It's like a Crocodile Dundee kind of knife. I'll never forget what she did. Those teenagers' eyes got huge as they stared at that knife being waved in their faces. And she looked at them straight in the eyes and said, "Now, you got something to say? Say it to me." And that's all I remember her saying. Nothing else! Before I could count to five those guys just turned very quietly and walked away. And do you know what? I never had another problem with those kids. That day my sister stood for me.

> At some unexpected moment in your life, you will need someone strong to stand up for you. That someone is the Lord.

In Jesus, we have an older brother who will stand up for us. When there is no one else and we are too weak to stand, the Lord will arise and stand up for us. Strong people stand up for themselves, but they also stand up for others. If you have been around long enough, you will know that there are moments when you just can't stand up. At some unexpected moment in your life, you will need someone strong to stand up for you. That someone is the Lord. He stands up for the oppressed, and broken and wounded.

The Lord Stood Up In Me

The Lord stands up *with* you. The Lord stands up *for* you. And, the Lord stands up *in* you. Have you ever awakened after a miserable night and just felt like you could not face another day? The pressures of life are squeezing you into an uncomfortable place, and you just don't know how to escape. You do not have the strength or the wisdom to go on. I have been there. There have been moments when I sat on the side of the bed after waking up and wondered how I would go on. The demands on my time and my life seem insurmountable. I contend with the responsibilities of running a worldwide ministry and, at times, feel weak and incapable of going on.

I don't know how you deal with these feelings. Maybe you are more spiritual than I am. Whenever I get in those moments, I go into deep self-contemplation, what some call "navel watching." But, inevitably in those moments of weakness, I will start praying and worshiping, and I begin to feel something rising up in me. At that time, I am reminded that I am not alone. There is One who stands up inside me.

He'll stand for me, but He'll also stand up in me at the time in my life when I think I can't do this anymore. I can't make it. I cannot go on another day. I can't face those people again. I can't get on that stage again. I don't want to see another microphone. I don't want to hear another song, and I don't want to hear another, "How you doing?" That's when He will stand up inside me.

What do you do? You start where you are and gradually your eyes will turn inward and upward. You begin to realize that there is a rising that is starting. He'll start rising up. And pretty soon your faith starts to rise. Pretty soon that faith starts to build.

I'll sit there for a while and then, I'll start thinking about all those things that God's brought me through. I'll start thinking about all the stuff that I've dealt with in my life. And I'll say, "Yeah, I remember I was in the hospital in Biloxi. Nobody knew I was there. I remember that all night flight to Hong Kong. Nobody knew where I was. I remember standing in the parking lot on Sixteenth Street, St. Petersburg, Florida, and it was the first time I went back to look at the building that I used to live in. I remember that closet I lived in. That building's gone. It's an empty lot now. It's all gone. Only a memory is left. I went looking for my youth pastor who taught me how to hand out tracts and witness to people. I found out he was in prison for attempted murder. I go back to Ft. Smith, Arkansas where my home pastor's buried. All of these experiences remind me of all that the Lord has brought me through. He did not deliver me *out* of it. He delivered me *through* it.

But when you think, *I can't do it another day*, He said He'll stand with you. He'll stand for you. But then, He'll stand up in you. And as the Lord begins to rise up in you, as that faith begins to build you up so that you can stand up and say, "Yeah, I can do it again today. I can do it one more time. Not in my strength, not in what I have, because I don't have anything left." As He rises up in me, I get my second wind. A new burst of spiritual strength invades my weakened body, all because the Lord stood up in me.

Purpose Is Always Resisted

Notwithstanding the Lord stood with me, and strengthened me; that by me the preaching might be fully known, and that all the Gentiles might hear: and I was delivered out of the mouth of the lion.

—2 Timothy 4:17

That all the Gentiles might hear: and I was delivered out of the mouth of the lion. At the point of your most intense conflict, you will find your greatest opportunity. It is so important to understand this truth. Many people fall just before they experience their greatest victory. At the moment of an unveiling of your purpose, you will experience great resistance. In his book, *Do the Work*, Stephen Pressfield describes this insidious enemy, called Resistance. "Resistance will tell you anything to keep you from doing your work. It will perjure, fabricate, falsify, seduce, bully, and cajole. Resistance is protean. It will assume any form, if that's what it takes to deceive you. Resistance will reason with you like a lawyer or jam a nine-millimeter in your face like a stickup man."[4]

> I don't trust anyone who doesn't have the scent of smoke on them. We are prepared for our purpose by the things we have had to endure.

Purpose is always resisted. In order to enter into your purpose, you must allow the Lord to rise up in you and overcome that which resists the manifestation of that purpose. The harder the resistance you experience, the more important the mission. The most successful people have known trials. They have known conflict, experienced resistance, struggled and they have been through the fire. I don't trust anyone who doesn't have the scent of smoke on them. We are prepared for our purpose by the things we have had to endure.

The list of things that Paul had to endure is very long, even being delivered from the mouth of a lion. You don't pull something out of a lion's mouth. That mouth is like a vice. Those jaws are so strong they will break a bone. To get out of the mouth of a lion you need a miracle. If you have never been in a place where you need a miracle, then you will never know what it means to have the Lord stand up with you, for you, and in you. The life you live and the message you speak must be backed up by the fire you have walked through. That's what it means to be a testimony, a witness to the glory and the power of God. It just isn't a message you speak. It must be backed up by your life. That's the power of a testimony.

So, what did Paul learn after all those years? What did he want to teach the young preacher? You'll never make it in the ministry and life, unless you learn this. He'll stand with you, guaranteed. He'll stand for you when you can't stand anymore. But He'll also stand in you when you feel like you can't make it another day. When you look back at all the things He's brought you through, you will be able to say, "Christ in me, the hope of glory." The Gentiles heard the message because someone fought against the resistance and experienced God standing with them, for them, and rising up in them.

Chapter 3

Compassionate Leaders: God in the Hands of an Angry Sinner

He is greatest whose strength carries up the
most hearts by the attraction of his own.[1]

Thousands of books have been written on the topic of leadership. Everybody has an idea of what leadership is and the qualities that make a good leader. I have often asked myself the question, "Who is qualified to be a leader?" In answering this question, the tendency is to define leaders according to their potential gifts and abilities. Potential based upon gifting does not necessarily segue into an effective leader. Leaders are not born; they are made. Having a position does not guarantee that you are a leader. Gift without character is a very bad equation for resolving the leadership problem.

There are many things that we can say about great leaders. Great leaders build their leadership around a vision, a goal, rather than around themselves. Their communication, confidence and commitment to the task will attract others to the cause. They lead by example more than by command. They are not bosses. They are leaders. They lead by example, not by force. They plough through and rise above their weaknesses and failures. Above all, they lead with their heart. Their compassion provokes response. Great leaders are compassionate leaders.

There are many great leaders in the Bible but, for me, one stands above the rest. That one is Moses. I've been studying the life of Moses for a very long time. In many ways, I think he is one of the most misunderstood characters in the Bible. His life is painted with contrasting colors of triumph and tragedy, as well as rejection and recognition. As a baby, he was adopted by Egyptian royalty, but became an outcast when he killed an Egyptian because of his anger at how the Jews were being treated. The Egyptians and his own people rejected him and his leadership was often challenged while Israel was in the desert.

Moses lived in Midian for forty years until his confrontation with God at the burning bush. His own insecurity almost sabotaged his call. We all know the story of how he and Aaron defied the Egyptians and led his people out of Egypt. We know the deliverance they experienced at the Red Sea. In spite of the greatness of this man, his life had its shortcomings.

You may have had to deal with your own deficiencies. You think because of your own weaknesses, God could never use you. Listen to me. Your imperfections in life, where you were born, how you were raised, and personal weaknesses, none of these things disqualify you from being a leader. If they did, then Moses certainly would not have been chosen. Paul's words ring true here. *But God hath chosen the foolish things of the world to confound the wise; and God hath chosen the weak things of the world to confound the things which are mighty* (1 Corinthians 1:27).

Many scholars believe that Israel's deliverance at the Red Sea was Moses' defining moment. I do not agree with that. He dealt with his weaknesses for most of his life: anger, insecurity, disobedience, fighting against God, making excuses, and other things that should have disqualified him. These imperfections followed him as he led Israel into the desert. It is when we get to Exodus 32 that we find that one defining moment in the life of Moses.

In this chapter, Moses was placed in a very uncomfortable position between Israel's idolatry and God's anger. The great loser was about to become the great leader. The one who needed Aaron to speak to the Pharaoh on his behalf was now boldly challenging God on behalf of Israel.

Sinners in the Hands of an Angry God

In the 1740s, like a great flash flood, the waters of the Great Awakening spread throughout New England. Hearts were set ablaze by the power of the Gospel. At that time, Jonathan Edwards was a pastor in Northampton, Massachusetts. He had become the pastor of a church that was, formerly, pastored by his grandfather. Ben Franklin, who made a lot of money printing the sermons of George Whitfield, spoke these words concerning this great revival. *"From being thoughtless or indifferent about religion, it seemed as if all the world were growing religious, so that one could not walk thro' the town an evening without hearing psalms sung in different families of every street."*[2]

In July 1741, theologian Jonathan Edwards (1703-1758) accepted an invitation to preach at the neighboring town of Enfield, Connecticut. He decided to preach the same sermon that he had preached in his own church, a sermon that had little effect on his congregation. His sermon, "Sinners in the Hands of an Angry God," would become one of the most well-known sermons of all time.

It is reported that Edwards' preaching style was less than impressive. He read his sermons in a quiet voice and with no theatrical antics, a style that he was opposed to. But the power and presence of God were so strong in that service that people were dramatically impacted by his word. Edwards used the words of Deuteronomy 32:35 as his prime text. "Thy foot shall slide in due time." Here is a little taste from the sermon he delivered that day:

"The God that holds you over the pit of hell, much as one holds a spider, or some loathsome insect, over the fire, abhors you, and is dreadfully provoked; his wrath towards you burns like fire; he looks upon you as worthy of nothing else, but to be cast into the fire; he is of purer eyes than to bear to have you in his sight; you are ten thousand times so abominable in his eyes as the most hateful venomous serpent is in ours."[3]

The conviction of the Holy Ghost was so strong that men were holding onto their chairs attempting to keep from falling back. Stephen Williams, a colleague of Edwards who was present on that historic day, said that the shrieks were piercing and amazing.[4] The message was so vivid that he was interrupted many times before finishing the sermon by people moaning and crying out, "What shall I do to be saved?"

Williams went on to recount that at the end of the meeting, after the wailing and crying had come to an end, that the power of God was seen and was amazing and astonishing. After a final prayer, they descended down from the platform, spent some time talking with the people, sang one more hymn, prayed and released the people. It was a day that would fuel the fires of that great awakening that had already started.

A Defining Moment

We could reverse the Edwards' sermon title to "God in the Hands of an Angry Sinner." It is all a matter of perspective. Moses' encounter with God on the mountaintop gives us an entirely different point of view on the relationship between God and man. Everyone has a timeline in their life that shows upward spikes of great consequence and downward spikes of failure and weakness. Sometimes, we are angry with God because we don't get what we want. We lash out at God in an attempt to cover our own shame and guilt.

> There will come a defining moment in your life where you will come to understand that failure does not disqualify you. Failure is never final.

The point that I want to make here is that there are moments in our lives where life as we know it becomes redefined. Life and death, victory and defeat hazardously hang in the moment when we are forced to make a decision on what we are going to believe about our life. You cannot constantly define your life by its moments of imperfection.

There will come a defining moment in your life where you will come to understand that failure does not disqualify you. Failure is never final. The standards that are used to qualify leaders are just ridiculous. There are so many leadership conferences and seminars and most of them are not helpful at all. We need to see leadership through God's eyes. As Paul said, God chooses the ones that others would reject. He chooses the ragamuffins of this world. Few could live up to those high standards held up for the *perfect* leader.

Moses on the Mountain

After the children of Israel had crossed over the Red Sea, they traveled south, through the Sinai Peninsula and along the Gulf of Suez until they finally arrived at the plains surrounding Mount Sinai. This is the historic and holy site where Moses received the Ten Commandments. The Decalogue, as it is called, was a set of biblical principles relating to ethics and worship and became the guiding principles for Jews and Christians.

An interesting side note, the Commandments were written on both sides of the tablets, as stated in Exodus 32:15, probably giving it a double confirmation. *And Moses turned, and went down from the mount, and the two tables of the testimony were in his hand: the tables were written on both their sides; on the one side and on the other were they written.* These were the words of the law that would set Israel apart from all of the surrounding nations. It is the written covenant that makes Yahweh the God of Israel and Israel becomes God's Chosen People. From this point forward, Israel, of all the nations of the earth, would have a unique relationship with God.

> In the silence of the mountain, we are more susceptible to the voice of the Spirit.

This momentous event was initiated in Exodus 19:3 where Moses went *up* into the mountain and God called out to him. When God is preparing a person to move into a defining moment of his or her life, He always brings them to a higher place.

There are many illustrations of this truth in the Scriptures: Noah on Mount Ararat, Abraham on Mount Moriah, David on Mount Zion, Elijah on Mount Carmel and Jesus on the Mount of Transfiguration. A mountain-top experience, as we call it now, is usually characterized by some human encounter with God where revelation and refreshing are experienced. Climbing the mountain, we rise above the fog of religious activity in the valley. In those moments we can see beyond the fray, the fracas and the foolishness of life in the lower places. While in the valley of "hustle and bustle," we are distracted by the daily responsibilities consuming our life. As we begin to make our trek upward, the voices of "do this, do that" are silenced. In the silence of the mountain, we are more susceptible to the voice of the Spirit. Above the pollution that permeates life in the city, one gets a new set of eyes to see the invisible and to see life from a new perspective. It is in those moments that our lives get defined in a brand new way.

Unusual Request: Leave Me Alone

*And the LORD said unto Moses, Go, get thee down; for **thy** people, which **thou** broughtest out of the land of Egypt, have corrupted themselves.*
—Exodus 32:7 emphasis added

Life cannot, forever, be lived on the mountain-top. At some point, you must come down. On descending the Mount of Transformation, Jesus had to deal with the father of a demon-possessed child and the anger generated by the crowd at His disciples' inability to heal the child. The majesty of the moment on the mountain was broken. Descending the mountain, He knew that He must return to the valley of pain and unbelief.

Life is like that. The times of refreshing in the high places prepare us for life in the low places. What we received on the mountain will be tested in the valley. Oswald Chambers once said that the test of mountain-top experiences is when you are "in the soup" of actual circumstances. For every experience on the mountain, there will be wonderful things seen and learned. For every experience on the mountain, there will be an ensuing experience in the valley. For every experience in the valley, there will be a new lesson. I have learned that both the mountain and the valley are great teachers. On the mountain a truth is revealed and in the valley that truth is tested.

The twelve chapters leading up to chapter 32 deal with the establishment of Israel as a nation based upon the laws of God, a tabernacle for worship, and a priesthood. At the conclusion of these divine directives, the voice of God interrupted that glorious moment with this anger-filled command: "Moses, get yourself down..." *Uh, oh! This cannot be good.* God told Moses that *his* people that *he* led out of Egypt have corrupted themselves. God deliberately changed the possessive pronoun. I can hear Moses thinking, *What's this 'my' people? What about all those wonderful plans You just gave me?* God was saying that they were not His people anymore. "Moses, they're your people." Because of their sin, God has distanced Himself from the people. I can imagine Moses being stunned by these words. God went on to tell him that on the verge of becoming a great nation, they have already violated His law by building a golden calf for worship. God ended the conversation by telling Moses to just let Him be. "Let me stew in My own anger before I destroy them." One last thing, God told Moses that after He destroyed them, He would make a great nation out of Moses.

I can't tell you how many times I have walked out of our main office and just gone upstairs and closed the door. I have become so frustrated watching people destroy their lives. And there's really not a thing you can do. I know that. We all know that. You can't change people. God is the only one who can. You can do what you can do, but after that, it's up to Him to do the work. And then, it's up to them to respond. And that's very hard. It's very hard for me still, after all these years. You would think that after a while I would get used to it. I hope that I never do. I hope that I never become so callous that I stop caring.

So, there was Moses! Standing before God, he knew that he could not defend the actions of these people at the foot of the mountain. They have the potential to become the greatest nation on earth. They have been selected by Yahweh to be His special people, and they are there dancing around a golden calf. Are they nuts? What have they done?

So, God came back at him again with this unusual request: "I've seen these people. Now, leave Me alone!" *Leave You alone? Why did God say that?* Because this was a one-sided conversation! God was doing the talking, as Moses stood before Him in dead silence.

> God uses the experiences of life to cause us to see that there is much more inside of us than we ever knew.

Well, for a moment, it was a one-sided conversation. But, I think God was just setting Moses up. God does those kinds of things, you know? Moses had just entered into a test, and he didn't know it. Life is sort of like that. He wanted to see what Moses was made of. He wanted to see if Moses really had the capability of defending his people before God. God was trying to get Moses to see something in himself—something that he never saw in himself. God uses the experiences of life to cause us to see that there is much more inside of us than we ever knew.

The scene was set. God had vented before Moses. He was angry with these stubborn, ungrateful people. In essence, God said, "Moses, let's just kill them all and start all over again." He was upset. He had voiced His displeasure. Now, He was quiet. God was done with His venting. Moses was there in the stillness of a very uncomfortable moment. He probably needed to say something. The angels were looking on. All of history was waiting for this momentous moment to unfold. Moses had the opportunity to make a difference. It looked like something could be done. What will Moses do? What will he say?

Compassionate Reply: Moses Besought the Lord

What was Moses to do? He was faced with a critical moment, a defining moment. A decision must be made. On one hand, he can be quiet and let God destroy Israel and start all over. Not a bad idea after all Moses had gone through with Israel. Or, should he stand up to God and defend Israel?

> There's nothing great about being in the middle of two opposing people.

I don't know what I would do if I was on the receiving end of that conversation. Moses didn't want this job in the first place. It was God's idea, not his. Even after he gave in to God's call, it was not really a great job. Leading these people had been a real pain.

Moses was standing alone. He was forsaken by his people. They didn't want him. They thought that after he'd left and gone he wasn't coming back. So, they enticed Aaron into building a golden calf to worship. Now, they'd gotten themselves in a real mess with God and put Moses in the middle. There's nothing great about being in the middle of two opposing people.

God finished speaking. There was that awkward moment of silence, the pregnant pause. In the way this is written in Hebrew, it would appear that there is this break in the conversation. God had said His piece. Pause! How would Moses respond? I am sure that Moses was thunderstruck and shaken, not knowing how to respond in this tense-filled moment. He knew God was right. There was no logical defense for Israel's actions. However, he had to do something or some very bad things were going to happen.

Finally, Moses spoke. *And Moses besought the LORD his God, and said, LORD, why doth thy wrath wax hot against thy people, which thou hast brought forth out of the land of Egypt with great power, and with a mighty hand?* (Exodus 32:11). He beseeched God, appealing, imploring, pleading, adjuring, and petitioning God to reconsider.

The New American Standard says that he *entreated* the Lord his God. The New International Version says that he *sought the favor* of the Lord his God. Young's International says that he *appeaseth* the face of Jehovah his God. One last translation by Everett Fox says, "Moshe *soothed* the face of YHWH His God, he said: For what reason, O YHWH, should your anger flare against Israel…"[5]

Moses gathered up his courage and sought to calm and soothe God, beseeching Him for favor in this crucial moment. The man who has been brutally abused by the people of Israel on various occasions now must become their defender! Moses' defense began by reversing God's words. He reversed those possessive adjectives and put them in their proper place. These are YOUR people that YOU brought out of Egypt. It was YOUR plan to make them a great nation.

He was reminding God of this established and celebrated truth. "They are still Your people!" God was offering Moses a pretty good deal. Here's the deal: We can destroy these ungrateful people, and I will start over with YOU. That isn't a bad idea.

But, Moses didn't even give it a second thought. In total unselfishness, he turned it back around, put it back in God's hands and said, "No, they're Your people. You did this. You brought them out." This is his defining moment. His compassionate response unlocked the mercy of God. His heart was compassionately in tune with God's people and he petitioned God to reconsider the actions He was considering. Moses became the man in the gap. The intercessor was standing his ground on behalf of the children of Israel. He had passed the test. He'd won the heart of God.

Critical Reason: They Are Your People

*And Moses besought the L*ORD *his God, and said, L*ORD, *why doth thy wrath wax hot against thy people, which thou hast brought forth out of the land of Egypt with great power, and with a mighty hand? Wherefore should the Egyptians speak, and say, For mischief did he bring them out, to slay them in the mountains, and to consume them from the face of the earth? Turn from thy fierce wrath, and repent of this evil against thy people. Remember Abraham, Isaac, and Israel, thy servants, to whom thou swarest by thine own self, and saidst unto them, I will multiply your seed as the stars of heaven, and all this land that I have spoken of will I give unto your seed, and they shall inherit it for ever.*

—Exodus 32:11-13

Moses gathered his thoughts and was ready to speak. He was unprepared to enter a verbal wrestling match with God. His words had to be calculated in a way to elicit a positive response. His courage to speak would surface from the compassion in his heart. Moses had his own issues with the children of Israel, but he ascended above these concerns, stood in the gap and appealed to God. In an effort to save Israel from God's wrath, he offered God three critical reasons why He should relent.

There's a generation to be restored. He reminded God that these are HIS people. He is the one who chose Israel, delivered them from Egypt and was leading them to the promise land. This present generation may be lost. However, they have children that are coming up behind them. There's a generation that has to be restored and saved. You just can't kill everybody. There's got to be a restoration plan that will preserve the next generation.

Israel is God's people, for whom He has done so much. Surely God would not now destroy them, and undo His own work. You just can't kill everybody! He implored God to reconsider what He was about to do and think about the future. Maybe it was too late for this generation, but have mercy on the next generation. Moses pleaded with God to fulfill His purposes for Israel in the next generation. Moses reminded God that He had invested too much in this heavenly plan to turn back now.

There's a reputation to be preserved. As a lawyer before the judge, Moses now presented his next defense on behalf of his client, Israel. He appealed to God's reputation. If God carried out His plan, then Egypt would speak evil of this divine action and say that God brought them out of Egypt to destroy them in the desert. What was Moses saying here? He was saying that God's reputation among the nations of the earth, especially Egypt, was on the line. The Egyptians had witnessed the power of Israel's God as He delivered them, now what would they think if God kills them in the desert? What kind of God is that? Moses appealed to God to reconsider and think about his reputation.

Did God need someone to defend Him? Maybe He did. Maybe He does more than some of us think He does. Moses said, "Hey, Your reputation's on the line here. If you pull the plug on Your plan, Your enemies are going to ridicule You." Moses tried to make God understand that His reputation was at stake.

I think we need to let our lives defend the nature of God. In some ways, Moses had taken on the forgiving nature of God. He was trying to reflect back toward, as in a mirror, His own character. If He's real and He is within us, then our nature and our character should take on His nature and His character. Moses put a mirror before God to help Him see that if He destroyed Israel, He would be acting out of character and His image would be ruined.

There's a promise to be fulfilled. Determined to win this argument, Moses finalized his defense with one more crucial point. Moses had pleaded with God to consider the *future* of Israel. He had entreated God to reflect on the *present* moment and how His actions would cause Israel to speak ill of Him. Now, we have his final argument. He implored God to consider the *past*. He reminded God that the promises made to Abraham, Isaac, and Jacob would be revoked and withdrawn if the nation were destroyed and a fresh start made.

God had made a promise, and Moses pressed that memory upon Him, reminding Him that those promises were made and could not be rescinded. Those patriarchs acted upon those promises. They made sacrifices. They obeyed God. They committed themselves to those promises. How could God go back on His word to them? Moses reminded God and challenged Him to reconsider, based upon His own promises to make a nation from them.

God is a Redeemer. He knows how to make the best out of the worst situation. Moses knew that, and if God would reconsider based upon His past promises, the scandal in the valley could be reversed and a promise salvaged.

Unusual Result: God Repents

And the LORD repented of the evil which he thought to do unto his people.

—Exodus 32:14

The defense rested! Moses had finished his arguments. Now, God must render His decision. The Bible says that the Lord repented. This verse has caused a lot of theological debate over whether God changes His mind or not. Malachi 3:6 says, *For I am the LORD, I change not.* In the light of Malachi's words, how can we interpret these words in Exodus? If we interpret these words literally, without understanding anthropomorphic language, it does seem to be a contradiction, a conflict in God's nature. How can God repent?

The King James Bible's use of the word *repent* creates the confusion. You have to understand the word in the context of its Hebrew word, *nahum.* Nahum does not mean a change of thinking. It's not a change of character, but it's a change of action. He changed His actions. His character/nature remains the same. There was no sin to repent from. There was no character flaw. He saw, He heard, He listened, and He changed his decision. This abrupt course change was instituted because of one man who acted as a mediator and an intercessor. Thirty-eight times in the Bible, a mediator stood before God on behalf of the people. Like Moses, Amos stood up for Judah in a similar fashion.

Thus the Lord GOD showed me, and behold, He was forming a locust-swarm when the spring crop began to sprout. And behold, the spring crop was after the king's mowing. And it came about, when it had finished eating the vegetation of the land, that I said, "Lord GOD, please pardon! How can Jacob stand, for he is small? The LORD changed His mind about this. It shall not be," said the LORD.
—Amos 7:1-3 NASV

Samuel, Abraham, and many of the prophets stood in the gap for their people. In times of national trouble, God always looks for someone to stand in the gap. He puts the fate of a nation and the reputation of His character into the hands of someone who can be trusted, who will pass the test. Moses got it. He understood the situation and responded in a way that would reverse God's decision. God smiled. Moses performed exactly how God had hoped and expected.

As we said earlier, this was Moses' defining moment. At this particular time in his life, he averted a devastating detour in God's plans for Israel and preserved Israel's future generations. Moses did not allow his personal feelings to interfere with his interaction with God. If it had been me, that would have been tough. Believe me, the children of Israel were not the easiest people to lead. Moses had his issues with them. But, in this historic moment, he played out his role perfectly. He was God's man for the moment.

Moses was able to step out of the emotion-packed moment and speak with compassionate wisdom. Juxtaposed between a bunch of knuckleheads in the valley and a God about to wipe them out, Moses was able to navigate through a whirlwind of emotions and thoughts and do the right thing. He knew it was not about him. It was about the interests of those around him.

I have worked with a lot of young people over the years who are trying to find their place in ministry. Unfortunately, too many of them are too self-absorbed and only seek out what works best to their advantage. Over and over, I have had to tell them that it is not about them. It is about the ones they are called to serve. Moses was not trying to "find his ministry." He wasn't trying to establish his authority. Moses was consumed with one thing: serving God's purposes among His people. Though they could be irritating at times, Moses loved his people. He stood with them in the good and the bad. He sacrificed himself on their behalf. His love trumped his frustration with their failure and inconsistencies. He wasn't concerned about his reputation. He didn't want his name memorialized with Abraham, Isaac and Jacob.

> Great leaders seize the moment of opportunity, in spite of their own weaknesses.

One person can make a difference. That person is not necessarily defined by their background, their education, their skills and abilities. They are not guided by their own quest for greatness. They are not consumed by the need for recognition and affirmation. Their vision is more focused toward others, rather than themselves. They are driven to serve, rather than be served.

Great leaders seize the moment of opportunity, in spite of their own weaknesses. Moses struggled with his own personal issues. But, when that one defining moment presented itself, he rose above the complexity and impossibility of that single moment and made history. The question begs an answer for all of us. Will we recognize our defining moment and how we shall respond? Only you can determine the answer to that question.

Chapter 4

The Acceptable Sacrifice:
A Broken and Contrite Heart

God doth not only prefer such an one, as has been said, before heaven and earth, but he loveth, he desireth to have that man for an intimate, for a companion; he must dwell; he must cohabit with him that is of a broken heart, with such as are of a contrite spirit.[1]

Johon Bunyan (1628-1688) was one of the greatest English writers of the 1600s. He had very little traditional education, became a tinker (repairer of pots) like his father and served in the Parliamentarian army. Bunyan would continue to wander through life until his conversion. Concerning that conversion Bunyan wrote these words, "*By which I was made to see, both again, and again, and again, that day, that God and my soul were friends by this blood; yea, I saw that the justice of God and my sinful soul could embrace and kiss each other through this blood. This was a good day for me; I hope I shall never forget it."* [2]

During a time of persecution, imposed by the Church of England, Bunyan spent 12 years in prison for preaching without authorization. It was during those years of imprisonment that he wrote *Grace Abounding*, and several other lesser known books. It is believed that in the latter part of his first imprisonment he formed the ideas for his greatest book, *The Pilgrim's Progress*. The second part of *Pilgrim's Progress* was written on the back of milk bottle stoppers while in the Bedford jail. By 1688, over 100,000 copies of that classic book had been sold. It became the greatest allegory of all time.

The final book written by Bunyan was *The Acceptable Sacrifice*. The book was not published until after Bunyan's death in 1688. It is believed that this book is the culmination of the years of harshness that John Bunyan suffered. Bunyan spent a great deal of his adult life studying the Bible so that he might understand the heart of God. Without a doubt, this book expresses the heart of God and how He leans toward those of a broken and contrite heart.

When I first saw a copy of this book in Norway, I picked it up, looked through it, and ended up buying it. Before I purchased the book, I had preached a sermon called, "When a Sacrifice is No Longer a Sacrifice." Over the years, I have come to understand that God is attracted to those of a broken and contrite heart. This is the only acceptable sacrifice.

I spent a lot of time reading this book. It impacted me because it is where I am. It touched me in a way that was very different than any other book. The truth of Bunyan's carefully crafted words rang true to my own life. Not all sacrifices are acceptable to God. If they are offered up in pride with *strange* fire, they will not be acknowledged by God.

Rehoboam was a son of Solomon and became king following his father's death. Because of a dispute over excessive taxation, Jeroboam led a rebellion against Rehoboam which split the nation of Israel. Rehoboam remained as king over the Kingdom of Judah (Southern kingdom) and Jeroboam became the first king of the Kingdom of Israel (the Northern kingdom). Throughout his reign, the conflict continued.

In the fifth reign of Rehoboam, Shishak, the king of Egypt, invaded Judah and took many of the cities in Judah. When he arrived at Jerusalem, he cordoned off Israel preventing anything entering or leaving the city.

The third character we want to consider is Shemaiah the prophet. Shemaiah lived in Judah during the time of Rehoboam. Shemaiah had warned Rehoboam not to go to war against Israel and in obedience to his word he refrained from going to war. One of the lost books of the Old Testament is a book called the *Book of Shemaiah the Prophet*, which was a record of the time of Rehoboam's reign.

Even though Rehoboam had started out right, serving God as a godly king, something happened and the Bible says that he forsook the ways of the Lord. Throughout the times of the kings of Judah and Israel, whenever a king followed in the ways of the Lord, there was peace in the land. But, whenever they abandoned the law and followed other gods, they would be invaded by other nations. In whatever direction the king went, the people would follow. This is a great lesson for all those in leadership. The accounts of the kings, in the books of Samuel, Kings, and Chronicles, reveal what God demands from leaders. If they fail, a ripple effect of disastrous consequences is created.

Threat of Condemnation

And it came to pass, when Rehoboam had established the kingdom, and had strengthened himself, he forsook the law of the LORD, and all Israel with him. And it came to pass, that in the fifth year of king Rehoboam Shishak king of Egypt came up against Jerusalem, because they had transgressed against the LORD.

—2 Chronicles 12:1-2

After Rehoboam had strengthened his power in Judah, he forsook the law of the Lord, a very bad decision. You reap what you sow! Rehoboam saw trouble on the horizon. Shishak had left Egypt with a mighty army and entered into the land of Judah. The reports had reached his palace, and he prepared for the coming invasion.

> Most of our problems are foreseeable. No problem just suddenly appears.

Most of our problems are foreseeable. No problem just suddenly appears. Small issues will, eventually, become big problems. Most problems that can destroy you don't just crop up one day. A husband comes home one day and his wife tells him she wants a divorce. Don't tell me that there were no warning lights being flashed prior to this declaration. I don't care what issues you're dealing with. When a flashing red light of trouble arises, there are three things people usually do. 1. Ignore them and hope they go away. Believe me they will not go away. 2. We are so busy with other things that we miss the warning light. G.K. Chesterton once said that it isn't that people don't see the solution; they can't even see the problem. 3. We recognize the emerging trouble and act in a way to prevent further disaster. Now, what we do with them when we identify them is going to be up to you.

I have often said that prevention is better than intervention. The old Ben Franklin adage applies here: An ounce of prevention is worth a pound of cure. Too many people wait until an issue becomes a crisis, a hindrance becomes a habit, and a transgression becomes a travesty. If we allow problems to grow and fester, they always grow into full blown crises. Issues rise up. People are hurt. Relationships are jeopardized. Ministries are devastated. Why? Because some of us failed to see what was coming on the horizon. The reason why most of us have financial problems is because we don't monitor things in anticipation of what could be on the next horizon. Every once in a while something will sneak up, but for the most part it's fairly normal to be able to see things ahead of time.

Great leaders detect the smoke before it is converted into a raging fire. Shishak was rising up against the people of God. Rehoboam saw it. He knew what was going on, and he reacted to the threat of condemnation.

Point of Revelation

Then came Shemaiah the prophet to Rehoboam, and to the princes of Judah, that were gathered together to Jerusalem because of Shishak, and said unto them, Thus saith the LORD, Ye have forsaken me, and therefore have I also left you in the hand of Shishak.

—2 Chronicles 12:5

In the Old Testament, prophets are also called Seers. There is a reason they were called seers. They saw things before others saw them. Their point of revelation, many times, saved the kings of Israel. Shemaiah came along and told Rehoboam and the other princes that because they had made a decision to abandon God, then God would leave them to their own demise.

It always takes somebody in touch with God to bring reality to our attention. Have you ever noticed that? Why is that? Why is it that Nathan had to point that bony prophet finger in David's face and declare, "You are the man!" Why is it that it always takes somebody that's just a little bit more in tune with the Spirit of God to step in and say, "Hey, here's something that needs your attention." We don't always see clearly. There are moments when our spiritual vision is clouded by sin or situations.

People have spoken into my life who have helped me see things that I did not see. No one is exempt of the need to have someone who can speak to them in times of unconscious awareness of where we are in life. I believe in accountability and the need to surround ourselves with people we trust—people that we permit to speak into our lives. Don't ever be fooled by the thought that you don't need anybody. We all need somebody. That's why the relationships with people that you are close to is important. Who is speaking into your life? What are they saying? Do not avoid them. Do not reject them.

Shemaiah spoke to the people, and he spoke to Rehoboam. He warned them that Shishak was coming and they'd better be ready. Never presume that you are invulnerable. Your sin will leave an open door for tragedy to happen. You need to close that door.

Act of Demonstration

Whereupon the princes of Israel and the king humbled themselves; and they said, The LORD is righteous.

—2 Chronicles 12:-6

Shemiah had spoken. Clarity was brought to the situation. The enemy was revealed. Now, what would the people do? There are times when it takes a knock upside the head to get people's attention.

Why does it take a tragedy? Why does it take a financial catastrophe? Why does it take a broken relationship? Why does it take a breach of trust? Why does it take these kinds of things to bring people to the point of brokenness? Why does it take somebody losing a child in an accident to bring them to brokenness? Why does it take a failed marriage to bring somebody to the point of realization? Why does it take a severed friendship or a family that's been internally destroyed or a ministry that gets damaged? Why is it that we always wait till *after* a catastrophe to experience brokenness? You'd think we would be smarter than that. I have watched a lot of people go through so much before they finally get the point. Maybe, that is the only way we learn.

The truth might be found in Bunyan's words, "...*he wounds before he makes whole*." I don't think that genuine brokenness can be realized in our lives without being wounded. The subtlety of pride makes us think we are the commander of our circumstances and the sergeant of our soul. It is only when we are confronted with trials and tragedies that we understand that our only power is in the Lord. It is a paradox but it is true. The wounding will bring the healing.

"*They humbled themselves*." After the prophet delivered his word, it says they humbled themselves. The prophetic word did its work. The word had broken them. David had the same experience in Psalm 51. He had come to the place where he realized that he had sinned greatly before the Lord. In this chapter, he poured out his heart to the Lord, asking for grace and mercy. He now understood that it is not enough to make an outward sacrifice for sin. The true sacrifice is the sacrifice of a broken spirit. *The sacrifices of God are a broken spirit: a broken and a contrite heart, O God, thou wilt not despise* (Psalm 51:17).

A broken and a contrite heart, these are the sacrifices of God. Once we are broken, a sweet fragrance is released from our spirit. Charles Spurgeon put it this way in his exposition of Psalm 51:17, *A heart crushed is a fragrant heart.*[3] There is a story told in Mark 4 about Jesus being invited to the home of Simon the Leper. While there, a woman entered the home, approached Jesus, broke an alabaster box of oil and anointed Jesus with it. The fragrance of that pure spikenard filled the whole room. If the box was not broken, the fragrance could not be released. So it is with us, unless we are broken, the anointing fragrance cannot flow.

The Scripture says that Rehoboam humbled himself. He allowed it to happen to himself, because he made the choice to allow it to happen. He made the decision to permit the process to begin that would result in humility. He humbled himself. He bent himself down low. He submitted to the word and allowed himself to be broken by that word. Brokenness brings humility. You have to be emptied before you can be filled.

I wonder how many have ever let God break their heart. This is not religious jargon. This is not a rhetorical thought. This is a legitimate and critical question. The way you answer that question will determine your success in life. You don't just wake up one day and say, "I think I'm going to allow God to break my heart today." Normally, it takes a divinely crafted circumstance for that to happen. When God breaks the heart, something happens. Our perspective on life changes and a fresh perspective humbles us in the presence of God.

Not only is it a broken heart—it is now a contrite heart. Shishak was about to come in and destroy everything. A man of God spoke.

There was a point of revelation. But then, after the point of revelation, somebody had to act on it. There had to be an action. From the place of brokenness, change and healing come. There is a lamenting for the things we have done and a longing to correct and heal the broken places.

Make me to hear joy and gladness; that the bones which thou hast broken may rejoice (Psalm 51:8). What happens when a bone gets broken? What do you have to do to it? The doctor has to put it in its proper place and then set it in a cast. When you have a broken leg in a cast, you are totally disabled. And not just disabled, but you are unable to do those things which you were once able to do. That's where true change comes, when we realize that we are not the masters of our

> What God has broken,
> He will heal.

own fate. For the first time, we come into a confrontation with our own weaknesses. Once that realization is complete, healing can come. A broken heart can become a healed heart.

When God breaks the heart, you change. There is contrition and a humility that is now evidenced in your life. Before the brokenness, you trusted in your gifts, your education, your personality and your strength. Now, that you are broken, you live life in a new awareness of the need to trust God and you now rely on His wisdom and strength. You have been crushed by your circumstances, but you have been cured by His compassion.

After the crushing comes a re-creation. As in the creation of the world, God creates something out of your nothingness. From the emptiness, there comes a filling. From the brokenness comes a healing. What God has broken, He will heal. Now, the two can become one, God and man. Until you have been brought low, you can never ascend into the high places. Through the process of being broken, you now move into a new level of healing and usefulness.

A Time for Application

And when the LORD saw that they humbled themselves, the word of the LORD came to Shemaiah, saying, They have humbled themselves; therefore I will not destroy them, but I will grant them some deliverance; and My wrath shall not be poured out upon Jerusalem through Shishak. Nevertheless they shall be his servants; that they may know My service, and the service of the kingdoms of the countries.

—2 Chronicles 12:7-8

Shemaiah spoke the word. Rehoboam repented and humbled himself. Now, God would do His part. The word of the Lord came to Shemaiah. God rendered His decision. He would not allow them to be destroyed. However, they would be subjected to King Shisak so they might learn the difference between serving God and serving earthly kings.

God's word is His power. When He renders a decision, He will then activate and apply His word to the situation. The word of the Lord came. Though there might be moments of silence, God's word will come, and He will make His intentions clear. God is attracted to the broken heart and His voice will be heard in the depths of their hearts.

Is not my word like as a fire? saith the LORD; and like a hammer that breaketh the rock in pieces?

—Jeremiah 23:29

God's word is the heat and the hammer. It crushes the hardened heart and melts the steely soul. Also, the hammer of God breaks the walls that separate us from our divine purpose. Like a jackhammer, it breaks up the hardened concrete that keeps us from blossoming. The fire of God is a refiner's fire that purges away the impurities and imperfections and produces the finest silver and gold.

Some people respond quickly to the heat. The hammer is reserved for those who will not respond to the fire of His word. How hardened are you? Will you need the heat or the hammer?

God looks beneath all of our outward expressions of religious devotion and searches our hearts. He seeks to transform us until our hearts beat in tune with His heart. In his book, *The Roots of the Righteous,* American pastor and author A.W. Tozer (1797-1963) describes that spiritual process with these words: "The devil, things and people being what they are, it is necessary for God to use the hammer, the file and the furnace in His holy work of preparing a saint for true sainthood. It is doubtful whether God can bless a man greatly until He has hurt him deeply."[4]

Prepare Your Heart

And he did evil, because he prepared not his heart to seek the LORD.

—2 Chronicles 12:14

"He prepared not his heart." He slipped back into his old ways because he did not fix his heart—did not set his heart on seeking God. The crisis was over, the pressure was off, and Rehoboam reverted back to the old ways of living. Some people never learn. They will do anything

to get out of the fire, but when they are out the fire, they are easily seduced and return to the place that pride built.

He swapped hearts, trading a tender heart for a hardened heart. He had the opportunity to be a great king in Israel, but he lost that opportunity because he no longer sought the Lord. In Deuteronomy, we see a command that comes with a promise. *Ye shall walk in all the ways which the LORD your God hath commanded you, that ye may live, and that it may be well with you, and that ye may prolong your days in the land which ye shall possess* (Deuteronomy 5:33). The command is to walk in the ways of the Lord and the promise is that if they do follow Him, then they will prosper and prolong their days. Because Rehoboam did not walk in God's ways, he forfeited this promise.

> Through disappointments, through heartbreak, through setbacks, and through lack of trust, our hearts can become hard and cynical.

In Deuteronomy 10:16 we find the key to preparing your heart, *Circumcise therefore the foreskin of your heart, and be no more stiffnecked.* How do you prepare your heart? In order to prepare our hearts, we must allow them to be circumcised. Rehoboam had his heart softened during the conflict with Egypt. As time went along and the danger passed, he allowed his heart to become hardened. He allowed a fleshly covering to come around his heart. The foreskin of the heart is like scar tissue. Scar tissue replaces normal skin tissue when it is damaged and forms a hardness over the wound. This spiritual scar tissue is like an armor plate over the heart that will not allow natural growth to occur.

This tissue, as Deuteronomy describes, is a fleshly tissue. It is *of the flesh*. It prevents the heart from being sensitive to the Spirit and to others. It hardens into a scar. If we are not careful, the heart that has been healed by God can become damaged again. Over the years through disappointments, through heartbreak, through setbacks, and through lack of trust, our hearts can become hard and cynical.

The only way to heal a hardened, fleshly heart is through circumcision. A surgery is required. The infected skin must be cut away. If spiritual healing is to happen, at some point, the cynicism, the heartache, the pride and the pain must be cut away—removed. And that's why God says, "*Circumcise your heart.*"

You may not agree, but I believe that beneath every crusty old heart, there is soft tissue. If we can surgically remove the hardness that has formed over years of running from God, we will reach the heart originally made by God. I have worked with some of the toughest people you could imagine, some of the hardest people, hardened drug addicts, some of the hardest-hearted gang members, and some of the hardest criminals. When you get past the flesh, when you get past the façade, when you get past the hardness, you know what? There's still a little girl inside of every one of those women. There's still a little boy inside every one of those men. After all of that foolishness is cut away, there's a heart for God in there somewhere. When we choose to circumcise (and cut deep) the heart and tear away that covering—the veneer of a life we have built—we find a place where healing can begin.

Once we have circumcised the heart, we must daily watch over it so the scar tissue does not return. Rehoboam did not pay attention to his heart. Day by day, a resistance and a roughness began to form until his heart was hardened and his neck was made stiff. Pride and arrogance returned, and he did evil in the sight of God.

Hearts harden pretty easily. Subtle things creep in unaware. We choose to trust our own wisdom and strength. We abandon the place of prayer. Disillusionment is morphed into sarcasm. The accumulation of failure transforms faith into doubt. Before we know it, we have lost our heart to the dark side.

Rehoboam did not prepare his heart. The key to avoiding a hard heart and a stiff neck is to keep the heart pure. Guard your heart carefully. Be careful what you allow into the heart. Fix your heart on the Lord. Be determined that you will not be deceived. Avoid negativity that seeks to find a resting place in your heart. David gives us a clue as we seek, to help us avoid the corruption of the heart, in Psalm 57:7, *My heart is fixed, O God, my heart is fixed: I will sing and give praise.* Be resolute in your position. Honor God's word above the word of others. Let your heart be filled with worship, rather than the discord of unbelief and selfishness. Trust in the Lord and don't be propped up by your own illusions of greatness. If you prepare your heart daily, you will survive any test that is thrown your way.

> Trust in the Lord and don't be propped up by your own illusions of greatness.

Chapter 5

A Gifted Leader:
Your Gift is Your Calling

*"Your talent is God's gift to you. What you
do with it is your gift back to God."* [1]

know there are people who might disagree with this statement, but I believe it to be true. *The need is the call.* There are some who dogmatically say, "If you have had a direct audible voice, some kind of extracanonical, revelation experience that would direct you on what you should do, then you need to wait on the Lord and wait until that experience happens before you step out and do something." I don't believe that is true. I believe that the need reveals the nature of the divine call. Our gift gives us a clue that will unlock our ability to fulfill the call. The question is: How do I find my gift and calling?

"What is it that I need to do? What is it that I, as an individual or as part of a group, am called to do? It's always that question that plagues people. I know people who are fifty, sixty, seventy years old who still have not figured out what it is that they need to be doing with their lives.

Finding and doing the will of God is a challenge to so many people. It remains a mystery and a source of frustration. There is no lack of books on the topic but, too many times, they only add to the confusion and delay the process. That is why I say that the need is the call. Sometimes, we use the search for God's will as a way to avoid what is right before our eyes. In our search for God's will, we pass by many opportunities to serve others with our gift. The will of God manifests itself every day in the needs we see in others, and we are truly gifted to fulfill His will in those situations. The story of the Good Samaritan is a good illustration. The religious leaders passed right by that poor soul who was accosted by bandits and left lying in the ditch and needing help. The Samaritan had eyes to see the need and he answered the call but the religious leaders did not.

> Find your own gift and don't judge that gift by the gift that is in others.

Your gift is calling. Everybody has a gift and there is no doubt about that truth. Unfortunately, a lot of folks don't know how to recognize their gift or see the value of their gift. One of the complications in understanding our gift is how we judge ourselves in relation to others. Find your own gift and don't judge that gift by the gift that is in others. I like what Albert Einstein said relative to this thought. "*Everybody is a genius. But if you judge a fish by its ability to climb a tree, it will live its whole life believing that it is stupid.*"[2]

Once you understand what your gift is and the framework in which it works then you will move into the place where you need to be. Your gift is indicative of what your calling is. Find your gift! Find your calling!

Recognition of the Gift

Everybody wants what you have. Everybody needs what you have, but it is highly likely that you don't even know what you have. You have something valuable. You have a gift that you possess. When you recognize that you have that gift and you understand the purpose of the gift, a place will open for you to use that gift. A gift is to be used, not to place on a mantle to be admired.

"*Everyone has talent. What's rare is the courage to follow it to the dark places where it leads.*" If you give someone a gift, you would expect them to use the gift. God has gifted everyone. We don't necessarily know the places where that gift will be used. Sometimes, as in my situation, that gift is used in some pretty dark and dangerous places. The main point is that when a gift is given, it must be used. You are no longer your own. You no longer have privacy. You no longer have your own little life that you live. You will never get away from it. When you choose to give yourself to the body of Christ, you will be given to people who don't appreciate you or will criticize you. Don't let that discourage or prevent you from using your gift.

How do you find out what your gift is? There are a lot of practical tools and questions to use in identifying your abilities. What do you enjoy doing? What do you excel at? What comes easy for you? Ask others what they think your gifts are.

The only thing I ever enjoyed doing when I was young was driving the bus. That was my starting point for finding the other gifts in my life. Once you find what you enjoy doing, start doing it. As you get your life in motion, other gifts will appear. Sometimes, you just don't know the skills you have until you get into a place where they can be revealed. We discover our gift through work and interaction with others. We begin to see what we can do and what we cannot do. When this ministry started, I did everything. I was doing things I was not gifted for. Eventually, we had the finances to hire people who had the gift. Being an accountant would drive me nuts. I don't have the patience or skills for that kind of work. My gifts are situated in other places.

You receive a gift in order for you to give away a gift. This is one of the spiritual laws of discipleship. As Matthew 10:8 says, *Freely ye have received, freely give.* The cost you pay for your gift is a part of the process of building character. The gift must always accompany the character. Having a gift without character will create a whole world of problems for you.

We have already referred to the story of the woman with the alabaster box in John 12:3. Here is another hidden nugget from that story. The ointment that was in the box was called spikenard. "*In Jesus time, spikenard was very costly. The aromatic, oil is extracted from the fragile roots of the spikenard plant. In biblical times, it was transported from the sheep valleys of the Himalayas. The oil was sealed in amber boxes, to be opened only when it was ready for use.*" [3]

In order to extract the oil from the root, they cut the tree, chop up and crush the roots. In the crushing process, little drops of resin come out of the roots. At great cost, Mary then anointed Jesus with that precious oil. Before there was the gift, there was the crushing. There has to be a crushing process to recognize the value of what you have. That woman gave what would be the equivalent today of one year's pay, not just her tithe. Not one year of tithe. One year of her wages. And she broke it and anointed Jesus. She recognized that the only gift that she had was this precious oil. The gift had great value and so does your gifting.

Reservoir of the Gift

Every good gift and every perfect gift is from above, *and cometh down from the Father of lights, with whom is no variableness, neither shadow of turning.*

—James 1:17 emphasis added

Never forget that your gift comes from God. He created you, gifted you, anointed you, and uses you. He is the source. You are the recipient. Not only should we guard and use our gifts well, but we should also never forget where the gift comes from. It comes from above. Let me remind you that in the process of recognizing your gift, you'd better understand where it came from.

As success comes our way, it is easy to forget that God is the giver and we are the recipient. Pride sneaks in and the gift becomes an albatross around the neck. In Coleridge's poem, *The Rime of the Ancient Mariner,* we are introduced to the concept of 'albatross around the neck.' When the Mariner, a member of a mystic sailing ship, killed an albatross, the other crew members became fearful because the albatross was considered a good omen. The angry crew makes the Mariner wear the albatross around his neck.

> *Ah. well a-day. what evil looks*
> *Had I from old and young*
> *Instead of the cross, the Albatross*
> *About my neck was hung.*[4]

When we choose to forget that God is the source, we open up a very bad door and it eventually becomes a burden, rather than a blessing. Unfortunately, there are too many people in the Church who have forgotten this truth. If we are to walk along the humility road, we must always remember that God, out of His great grace, gifted us so that we can fulfill His purpose in our lives.

> **Find places where you can use and enhance your gift in service to others.**

God gives the gift and He expects you to give it back in service to Him, not for your gratification. Because He gave it to you, He wants part of it back. He expects you to use it. Your gift goes beyond what you get paid for. It comes from Him, but it's on loan and He expects you to develop the gift He has given you. "Can I be better?" "Can I improve my gift?" "Could I be better?" "Can I better develop my gift?" The answer to these questions is, "YES." Once you understand what your gift is, you develop it by using it. Find places where you can use and enhance your gift in service to others. Seek input from those who are more seasoned in your gift, so that you can be more skilled in your gift.

Regard for the Gift

Either what woman having ten pieces of silver, if she lose one piece, doth not light a candle, and sweep the house, and seek diligently till she find it? And when she hath found it, she calleth her friends and her neighbours together, saying, Rejoice with me; for I have found the piece which I had lost.

—Luke 15:8-9

The gift God has given you has great value and was given with a lot of thought. In return, we must treasure the gift because it comes with great cost. In Luke 15, Jesus tells three stories about the lost sheep, the lost coin, and the lost son. The value of the coin was not diminished because it was lost. If it was thrown in the trash, it would still have its same value. The coin retained its value, but the woman was the one who lost out.

We don't know how the coin was lost. The Bible doesn't say. It just got lost. Let's say a woman loses her wedding ring, you know how it feels. Panic sets in. She launches into a frantic flurry of activity to find it Like a mad person, she goes from room to room, frantically going through the dresser, looking under the bed, yanking the cushions off the couch and then goes out to her car to see if it fell off there. That is exactly what this woman did. You say, "Big deal, she still has nine others." I can tell you that the poor and miserable would not think that way. They don't take for granted the value of what they have. Unfortunately, too many of us in America do. We don't see the value of what has been given to us.

We do the same thing with people. We look at them and we make judgments and don't see their value. We judge them by the way they are dressed, the way they talk and where they live. We judge people harshly because we do not see the value in them. I know this all too well. I was judged wrongly when I was a kid. I was just a poor little boy with holes in his pants that nobody wanted. I was perceived as someone who had no value. We do it all the time. Be careful how you look at people. We all have a gift. We all have value. We need to see that, and we need to surround ourselves with people who appreciate our value.

Let's say that I got a brand new hundred-dollar bill. I can squish it, fold it, crumple it, or throw it in the mud. Guess what? It still remains a hundred-dollar bill and it still has its original value. It's the same way in life. Some of us have been squashed, thrown around, made mistakes, but our value is preserved. In fact, our life worth can be enhanced by the tragedies and trials we have had to overcome.

Here's another way to look at it. Suppose I have ten one-hundred-dollar bills. Those hundred-dollar bills add up to a thousand dollars. You don't call them ten hundred dollars. It is a thousand dollars. The value changes because of the set. It is now a set of bills. If you took one away, you wouldn't have a thousand anymore, would you? No, you'd have nine hundred. Consider this. There is power in a set. Why do you think that woman was so frustrated and upset when she lost one coin? She has lost one of a very important set. Now, she only has nine. There's still value in the nine, but it's not the same as the ten. If you break the set, you affect the value of the set, don't you? The value of the set increases in direct proportion to the number of individual units in the set.

> When a group of people come together with their gifts, there is greater value in the house. That is the power of the Church.

This is also a truism for the Church. When a group of people come together with their gifts, there is greater value in the house. That is the power of the Church. The power of the Church increases in comparison to the number of individual working parts that make up the whole. In 1 Corinthians 12:12 Paul writes these words concerning the Church, *For as the body is one, and hath many members, and all the members of that one body, being many, are one body.* The church is a set of members that make up the whole. All members are necessary and valuable for the Body to function properly. Never say that you are not valuable or important. This kind of negative thinking contradicts the truth of the significance of each member.

There's a difference between *sitting* in the house and *setting* in the house. You can be sitting in the house and not be set in the house. There are a lot of people who are lost in the house, like the coin was lost in the house. They haven't set or positioned their gift in a place where it can be used for the mutual good. If you are just sitting in the house, without using your great gift, you are diminishing the overall power of what the house could be. In order to adjust this situation, you must realign yourself with the house.

Here is a way to better explain what I am trying to say. I travel a lot. As you know, every country has its own currency. When I am at the airport ready to go to another country, I will exchange some of my American dollars into that country's foreign currency. Once my traveling is done and while I am at the airport, I go to the foreign exchange booth in the airport and switch the foreign money back to dollars. Quite a few times, I notice that the teller will always take those foreign bills and rearrange them so that they all face up in the same way. One day, I asked the lady why she did that. She told me that it is the only way they can wrap them. She said that they all have to be aligned. Light bulb! Those words shone a light on an important truth. In the house of God, we have many people with many gifts. As we have said, every gift has value and every gift must function in the Body. However, in order for it to function without chaos, each gift must be synched and aligned with the other gifts.

In 1 Corinthians 14, Paul is trying to correct an unruly situation in the Corinthian church. Everybody was using their gifts at the same time. People were speaking over one another and it was a muddled mess. Paul instructs them that the gifts are to edify the Body but that they must be shared decently and in order. There must be an alignment, an order, and a connection between the members and their gifts.

In this way, the Body can function in beauty and harmony. Everybody using their gift in synchronization with the other members of the Body will attract and influence others to approach and participate.

Requirement of the Gift

For unto whomsoever much is given, of him shall be much required.
—Luke 12:48

We have considered the *quality* of the gift. Everyone has been given a gift and that gift has great value, never to be diminished or desecrated. Now, we consider the *quantity* of the gift. God gives different quantities to different people. To those that are given more abilities, more is required. God evaluates each person according to the capabilities and the capacities that have been given them. Some are leaders over a family and some are rulers over a nation. The expectations adjust according to the realm of influence and giftedness you receive from God. You must not bury your gift as the one in the parable of the talents. You must retain and increase those gifts.

What are the requirements for retaining that gift? Every gift comes with a label: You are responsible to take care and nourish yourself and your gift. Here are some keys to enhancing your gift.

Feed your gift. How do you feed your gift? You practice it. You develop it. You work it. You read. You watch others. Like the old adage goes, "Practice makes perfect." You feed your gift by using your gift. You use your gift in service to others, not in promotion of yourself. The gift within you must not be disregarded—it must be demonstrated.

Another helpful way for feeding your gift is through reading. I am a lover of books. I have a library that is constantly expanding. The proper book will feed your gift. John Wooden was the most successful college basketball coach of all time. Wooden was an avid reader. He believed that books were an inexhaustible source of knowledge and wisdom and that *"a library of good books is a wise collection of friends, mentors, counselors, advisers, and encouragers."*[5] I make it my practice to constantly be studying and reading. I know that I can increase and hone my gifts by reading a variety of books.

> Keep balance in all that you do.

I can also feed my gift by watching and talking to other successful people. I watch what they do and say. I ask them questions about their life and success. In order to grow your gift, you must feed your gift.

Feed yourself. Not only do you need to feed the gift, you need to feed the keeper of the gift. You need to feed yourself. If your body fails, then there will be no way you can exercise your gift. Exercising and eating properly are important facets of keeping your body healthy. I am not saying you have to look like a bodybuilder. Don't do things in extreme. Keep balance in all that you do. That is my motto. However, it is important to take care of your body so that you can continue to use your gift.

Spend time around people that feed you. Choose people who are positive, upbeat people who value you, who value your gift, and that you can trust to speak into your life. In order to feed others, you must be fed.

Result of the Gift

A man's gift maketh room for him, and bringeth him before great men.

—Proverbs 18:16

Your gift will make room for you. I need for you to understand this. There's a big difference between the person and the gift. A person can have a great gift, but be a terrible person. If there is a great disparity between skill and character, it will be damaging to the individual and to others. Your challenge in life is to reduce the gap between who you are and what you do.

People will be attracted to your gift. If you are not careful, your gift will give the appearance that you are greater than you really are. It takes great grace to remain in the humble place, especially as your platform grows. People are attracted to those who help them, heal them, release them and serve them. This attraction can become a trap, so be prepared. Try to live your life in the constant awareness of who you really are. Don't let the crowds define you.

Your gift will open up doors. It will bring you to places and people you never imagined. However, never forget that there is a price to be paid. Your gift will cost you. My gift has cost me. I have no life of my own. I never will. It's over. It's done. I'm smart enough to know that. I can't go to an airport. I can't go out. Those days are over. There is a price to be paid for notoriety. Remember, that your life is not your own. You have been chosen with a purpose and gifted for that purpose. The gift brings results with it. Nonetheless, it will take great effort on your part to remain in the secret place of modesty and self-awareness.

When David killed Goliath, he was about to take a quantum leap from the private place to the public place. In the wilderness he had killed the lion and the bear. Having an audience when he defied and exterminated Goliath took him to new people and new places. A scruffy little teenager who just happened to be good with a slingshot will move from the wilderness to the palace. His gift opened a door for him.

The important key to David's surviving the transition is found in the friendship he had with Jonathan, the son of the king. If Jonathan had not mentored him, and if Jonathan had not taught him the ways of the palace, David would have been out of his depth. His gift made room for him. His gift opened the door. But, if somebody had not taught him and had not helped him, he would have been thrown out of that palace in no time flat. How many times have we seen people fail when popularity is thrust upon them? They did not understand the culture. They did not have the maturity to handle the media, the fans, or the money. Their illusions of grandeur will, eventually, get a dose of reality. Even though their gift made room for them, their character and their level of maturity could not keep them where God had placed them.

> You need people who can advise you, counsel you, stand with you, assist and support you.

When our gift unlocks doors and leads us into new realms of exposure and favor, we will need friends who can help us and support us throughout the process.

When you ascend into a higher position that brings admiration and applause, beware of wolves that come in sheeps' clothing. As Proverbs 30:15 says, "*Every leech has two daughters...*" There will be those who want to attach themselves to you and ride on the coattails of your success. As David had his Jonathan, you will need friends that you can trust and who have your best interest in mind. A good friend is hard to find, so when you find one, hold on to them.

You don't need friends who artificially try to sweet-talk you. You don't need flattery. You need friends who are as strong as you. Don't be intimidated by a friend who is smarter than you. They are also God's gift to you. You need people who can advise you, counsel you, stand with you, assist and support you. Smart people surround themselves with other highly gifted people and are not threatened by their gifting. A smart leader understands that they don't need to know everything. Great leaders will position great people into their lives. Andy Tibbs, Senior Lecturer in Advertising at the University of Gloucestershire described it best this way, "*Good people surround themselves with good people. Great people surround themselves with people far better than them. I thrive by having bright people around me, changing how I think about the world, challenging what the right next step is.*"[6]

I remember the first time I got my first big preaching opportunity. Pastor Tommy Barnett had asked me to speak at a pastors' conference in Davenport, Iowa. I was twenty-six years old. I thought I was big stuff in those days. I have never told this story, but it fits so perfectly. Tommy said, "I want you to teach a class." I was a bigger smart aleck then than I am now. I've tempered over the years and learned how to handle myself a lot better in situations like this. There were several hundred pastors at the conference, and I figured I knew a lot more than they did. Here is the rest of the story. I got up, and I made a fool out of myself. I said some things I should've never said. I knew that my gift opened that door for me, but I was not mature enough to know what to do once I got there. I wasn't smart enough, and I didn't have enough experience and, therefore, I made an idiot out of myself. My gift was greater than my character at that time. Not a good combination. There are some pastors out there who still think I am a numbskull. I have learned from my mistakes and that is one of the great keys to successful leadership. All of us make mistakes. It is how we learn from and correct those mistakes that are critical to our growth.

David's gift made room for him. But without a Jonathan, he would have never made it. Without a Jonathan in your life, you probably will make a lot of mistakes. All of us need people who will guard and strengthen us on our journey. When you get to that next level, here are some things that you need to consider. Watch and listen. Observe and learn. When you step into a different environment, it is important that you understand the culture and the people working in that culture. I'm still very, very conscious of my surroundings. When I'm in new surroundings that I'm unfamiliar with, I'll just stand off to the side and look and listen. I'll keep my mouth shut. I have been thrown into situations that I was not trained for, but I have learned how to read and respond to those situations. I have had great mentors who have taught me and stood with me. I have come to understand that it takes a lot more than just a gift to make you successful. You will need the *right* people to stand with you, and you will need to learn from your experiences. These are the things that make great leaders.

Chapter 6

The True Motivation: The Power of Love

Love is an all-powerful, all-encompassing concept. Love is unconditional. Love heals. Love conquers. Love is the purpose for human existence. Love is an activating thing. Love comes from a place where a person is pure of heart. Love is a choice.[1]

n this generation, love is a very enigmatic and misunderstood term. I don't know if we even have to define it, can define it, or are even capable of defining it. When you're young, love is a feeling. Young people think that they are in love because they have a feeling. They say that they have fallen in love. They are attracted to someone, usually by their looks and personality. For most, it is a feeling, an emotion. The problem with this is that just as easily as you have fallen in love, you can fall out of love. Love, on the emotion level, is a fleeting thing. True love must move and become more than a feeling. True love does not ebb and flow, like the waves of the ocean.

I remember that Huey Lewis classic song, *The Power of Love*. There have probably been more songs written about love than any other topic. Love can bring a person to their knees. It can unravel them. Love can break even the strongest. It tunnels its way under the hardness in our soul and reaches our heart and changes us.

Every once in a while in the Scriptures, we get a glimpse of a person's character and motivation. Secrets of the heart are revealed, either negatively or positively. You read about things that people did and see the outcome of their actions. God called Jonah to Nineveh but because of his prejudice, Jonah retreated in the wrong direction. Prejudice prevented him from responding to the call. Only after God's divine intervention, did he heed the call. What makes a person do what they do? What motivates and stimulates us to act in a certain way? Some people can rise above their pride and prejudice, and others cannot. The answer to those questions lie in the motivations of the heart.

For years I have preached and discussed the importance of motivation. Lou Holtz (1937-) , a former college football coach and television analyst, once said that this ability is what you are capable of doing and motivation is what you do. Motivation is the energy that creates action—the push that empowers choice. In order to be successful, everyone needs motivation.

Knowing the importance of motivation, we now ask this important question. What motivates people? Often I have wondered what motivated me and others to come to New York City. Why are we here? People have come from around the world to participate in what we are doing here. Motivation has a source. There is an internal drive to all motivation. Motivation can be supplied by various sources. Negative motivations can rise from a source of greed, pride, lust, fear, and desire for control. On the other side of the ledger, we can be motivated by concern, desire to serve, the needs we see around us, and compassion.

What becomes the real factor that moves people? I am in the last chapter of my life now, and I have been forced to face some choices. I have to be smarter about my life. A while back, while on a flight home, I had this conversation with myself, *I have some choices I need to make. Based upon my health and age, what exactly are those choices? What will move me or what will motivate me to make the right decisions?* I'm in the process. I am examining the motivations for those choices. I don't want to make those decisions based upon fear. What motivates me? I want to move forward, and I want to finish strong. All of us have to cross that invisible line that separates us from the complacency that kills and compassion that inspires.

Constrained by Love

For the love of Christ constraineth us; because we thus judge, that if one died for all, then were all dead.
—2 Corinthians 5:14

I have always been in love with words. I may be a lot more curious than the average creature. I just don't cruise through the Scriptures without going into port and studying what I just read. I have a need to know. The apostle Paul said he was constrained by love. What does he mean? *Constrained* is a very powerful word that paints a brilliant picture of the force that energized the apostle Paul. In order to interpret this picture accurately, we need to understand two things. What does it mean to be constrained? What is the constraining power?

The NIV translates the word *constrain* as "compels." The NASV translates the word as "controls." The Douay Bible translates the word as "presses us." The love of Christ is a pushing, constraining, and compressing force. It has the power of push and pull. It pulls us back when we have gone too far, and it pushes us forward in His desired direction.

> There is no doubt of God's love for us. It has been dramatically and forcefully demonstrated in the life of Christ.

Paul says that love is the constraining force. When you get married, you understand that you are bonded to that person. The mutual love between the man and the woman compresses them together in a way that they are compelled to live their lives together. There is no other one. Trying to interpret this verse correctly, we see that it could be Christ's love for Paul that constrained him or Paul's love for Christ that was the compelling force in his life.

There is no doubt of God's love for us. It has been dramatically and forcefully demonstrated in the life of Christ. In John 15:9, there is an answer to this question. *"As the Father hath loved me, so have I loved you: continue ye in my love."* Here is our answer. We have been affected and shaped by the power of Christ's all-consuming love. The love that has come to us from heaven has created in us a responding love for Christ. It is that responding love that is transformed as a constraining power in our lives. God's love for us has changed us and created in us a superseding love for Him.

The Love of Christ Pushes Me

Jesus' love for us pushes and thrusts us into the lives of others and into the harvest field. "The love of Christ constrains us." If we struggle with giving our best toward one thing, I believe that this internal resistance is a result of a lack of love. I think we can say this with confidence and not pervert the Scripture at all because Paul is saying, "the love of Christ." That love for Him does what? It pushes us. It pushes us toward something. It moves us. It presses us. I have noticed that those who are radically committed to a cause are misunderstood people. The reason being is that it is a very rare thing for people to be this way. Sometimes, their consuming passion and compassion put us to shame, and we avoid them.

The love *from* Christ and *for* Christ propels people into new dimensions of radical service for Christ. They are not just concerned; they are consumed. There's a big difference here. I think all of us are concerned, but how many allow their concern to consume them? Too many people in the Church are nine-to-fivers. Yes, they love God. Yes, they are concerned. However, their love and concern do not motivate them to action. It is one thing to faithfully go to church, but it is another thing to involve yourself in the needs of those around you. It is one thing to get involved in the church programs and it is another thing to get involved in God's program for the world. That's the difference between concerned and consumed. That's why it's much easier to just get involved in programs, rather than radical service for Christ.

Unfortunately, too much of our service becomes routine—action without passion. Do you know Sunday morning can be routine? It can happen in our relationships, as well. Husbands and wives can live together for a long time, and at some point, the passion disappears in their relationship. It happens with pastors and business people. You can be doing it so long that it can become routine, rather than remarkable. Life becomes cozy and predictable. We can become addicted to the comfortable. Only love can restore the passion of life.

Unless there is a foundation of love, you will not be able to survive the demands and intensity of any position in life. Doing the same thing over and over again can become monotonous and diminish the passion we once had. Trials and disappointment can wear away the original love we had for life. In these times, we turn to Christ and allow the fire of His love to reignite and reinvigorate us. You have to exit the comfort and disappointment zone and allow the pushing power of love to redirect you. By the power of that divine love, we take off our security blankets and reenter the adventure of following Christ.

The love of Christ pushes, propels, and places you in situations you would never imagine. I have been gripped by the power of that love. Everywhere I go, I tell people that I no longer make decisions. Most of them don't have a clue what I am talking about. They have not experienced that overwhelming and constraining love that forces me to follow His decisions for my life. Most of them are trying to figure out where they are going to lunch after the service, while I am trying to figure out where His love will take me next. My life is not my own. I have been captured by His love.

I live in two different worlds. I live in the world of preaching and traveling around the world. And I live in my precious world in New York. The traveling world pays for the world that I love in New York. It is in this world that love shines brightest. It's the love of Christ that constrains me.

I don't want to use the word *force* because I'm not sure that's exactly the right word, but I can't think of a better one. Love motivates me but it's even stronger than that. It's stronger. It's something that compels. It moves me to places and persons that I would not necessarily choose.

The Love of Christ Restrains Me

When Paul says, "The love of Christ constrains us," he means that the love of Christ restrains him. The love of Christ directs me and pushes me, but it also defines me and confines me. It propels and controls me. Like a mother eagle, it pushes us out of the comfortable nest. It also acts as the mother hen that gathers her chicks to her side. In some ways, it sounds contradictory, but it is not. They are simply different facets of how the same love for Christ impacts His followers. Not only does it move us toward something, but it pulls us away from other things. The love of God moves us toward service. It moves us with compassion. It compels us, if you will. The love that moves and pushes us also keeps us from the things that would hinder us from doing what we are called to do. Love has a gravitational tug, pulling us back into the circle of His intentions. It keeps us from wandering and straying into unintended places.

Although my old pastor committed suicide and it was so tragic, I still have great memories of him. His sermons had the greatest titles. I have one old tape of his that was done in 1977. I can't forget the title because I remembered that they put it on the marquee of the church. The title was: "If You Love God, You can do Anything you Want to Do." That title reflects the often-quoted words of Saint Augustine, "Love God, and do what you will." Augustine's homily included these words and gives us the proper context to this quote.

> There's total freedom in the love of Christ

"See what we are insisting upon; that the deeds of men are only discerned by the root of charity. For many things may be done that have a good appearance, and yet proceed not from the root of charity. For thorns also have flowers: some actions truly seem rough, seem savage; howbeit they are done for discipline at the bidding of charity. Once for all, then, a short precept is given thee: **Love, and do what thou wilt**: whether thou hold thy peace, through love hold thy peace; whether thou cry out, through love cry out; whether thou correct, through love correct; whether thou spare, through love do thou spare: let the root of love be within, of this root can nothing spring but what is good."[2]

These words are shocking to those who don't understand the powerful pull of the heavenly love. It is not a restrictive pull. There's total freedom in the love of Christ. This is NOT an excuse to do whatever YOU want. In order to properly understand this sermon title, you have to totally comprehend what *love God* means, as I have been describing it. If you really love Him, you will want to do only things that are pleasing to Him, because that's part of a love relationship. Within the parameters of love, there is a great freedom to act accordingly. A wife who loves her husband will find ways to please him and never give him a reason to mistrust her. She will go out of her way to find out what bother him and what pleases Him. The same truth holds true for husbands.

Permit me to tell you a personal story that illustrates this truth. I used to have a love affair with football, and I mean real football as it was played before this modern era of football. I loved the Steelers and the dynasty they had built back in the day. So, here's the story. I was preaching at a church on a Sunday morning and knew that I had limited time to catch the game between the Steelers and their arch rival, the Dallas Cowboys. It was a playoff game, and I would do anything to see that game.

I was watching my clock, plotting how I could make it work. I was desperate to see the game. I had calculated everything to get to the game on time. I was somewhere in a couple of time zones away from the start of the game and thought, *If I get out of there just right, then I will have time to find someplace that has a TV.*

I knew that after the church service, I'd have to go out and eat with the pastor, before I'd be free to find a place to watch the game. I had a small window between lunch with the pastor and the evening service at another church where I was scheduled to preach. Finally, I finished lunch with the pastor, said my goodbyes and got in my car. I drove as close to the next church as possible, looking for a restaurant that might have the game. Wouldn't you know it that the only place I could find was one of those half-bar, half-restaurant places.

I knew the game would be on the television in that restaurant. I squealed the brakes, made a quick turn and slid into a parking space. I jumped out of the car, locked it, and headed for the restaurant door. I opened it and looked for the television. There it was, situated inside the forbidden zone of the bar area. I stood right at the edge between the bar and the restaurant. I felt safe there. You know, when you're Pentecostal, there's about a two-inch gap of grace between you and safety. You are okay if Jesus comes. You still have some grace there. That is a little bit of sarcasm for you who are Pentecostal.

So I was watching the game, while at the same time looking at my watch. I knew how far it was to the church. My time was carefully calculated and I knew how much time I had left, before I had to leave. This might sound stupid to you if you're not that interested in sports, but, at that age of my life, it was life and death. I had to be there for the final minutes of this game. All of a sudden, I realized that my time had run out and the game was still going. I struggled because I wanted to see the end of that stupid game, but I thought *I can't do it.* I remember saying to myself, "Is this the way you're supposed to live? Has it come to this where I can't live like normal people?" Right then and there, it hit me.

I just nodded to myself and I thought, *That's why I do what I do and not many other people would do this because they want to stay home and watch a football game.* That's what separates some of us. There's nothing wrong with watching a football game. However, in that moment, I came to understand that the love of Christ constrains me. It moves you toward something. There are times that it will take you away from things, even things you love. We are both driven and hedged in by God's marvelous love. As hard as it is to understand, I find a great freedom in the constricting and liberating nature of that love.

The Love of God Contains Me

The love of God *pushes us*, the love of God *restrains us* and the love of God *contains us*. It pushes us toward something. It keeps us away from other things. And it keeps us in something. One of the great messages of the apostle Paul is that we are "in Christ."

> *Being justified freely by His grace through the redemption that is* **in Christ** *Jesus.*
>
> —Romans 3:24

> *There is therefore now no condemnation to them which are* **in Christ** *Jesus, who walk not after the flesh, but after the Spirit.*
>
> —Romans 8:1

*For the law of the Spirit of life **in Christ** Jesus hath made me free from the law of sin and death.*

—Romans 8:2

*Nor height, nor depth, nor any other creature, shall be able to separate us from the love of God, which is **in Christ** Jesus our Lord.*

—Romans 8:39

*Which He wrought **in Christ**, when He raised him from the dead, and set Him at His own right hand in the heavenly places.*
—Ephesians 1:20

*And hath raised us up together, and made us sit together in heavenly places **in Christ** Jesus.*

—Ephesians 2:6

*For we are his workmanship, created **in Christ** Jesus unto good works, which God hath before ordained that we should walk in them.*

—Ephesians 2:10

*But now **in Christ** Jesus ye who sometimes were far off are made nigh by the blood of Christ.*

—Ephesians 2:13 emphasis added

Our identity, inspiration and impetus are all found in Christ. We are contained in Him. When I wonder if I can go any further, this truth keeps me going. When I consider all that I have suffered, this reality makes me alive. When I think about all the pressures that surround me, the certainty of my position in Him gives me renewed courage to press through the pressures.

I've probably gone to church more than anybody should ever be in church in their whole lives. I have been in small gatherings and huge conferences. I have sat at private meals with some of the most renowned leaders in the body of Christ. I choose to be quiet in these kinds of private meetings and just eat the chicken and listen.

> In Christ's love, I find my strength, my passion, my vision, my direction, and all that defines my life.

But, all of this does not keep me going. It's not the chance to speak at large conferences. It's not the opportunity to hang out with famous people. It's not the recognition and notoriety. It is the love of Christ. I do all things because I am contained in His love. In Christ's love, I find my strength, my passion, my vision, my direction, and all that defines my life.

What keeps me going when I come home from a grueling time of travel and have to face a conflict between staff members? What compels me to get on another plane and travel to a foreign place? What keeps me from insanity when we lose a valuable staff member or the finances are running tight? It is the constraining and containing love of my Father. He envelops me, surrounds me and includes me in His marvelous, miraculous and mighty love. I cannot live without it.

Let's consider the man who wrote the words, "The love of Christ constrains me." Paul's portfolio of suffering is beyond imaginable. He was shipwrecked, beaten, left for dead, betrayed, imprisoned, surrounded by great peril, and persecuted by the Jews and the Romans. Where did he find the strength to carry on? What motivation impelled him to the most dangerous places? What empowered him to reject the easy road and embrace the sufferings of Christ? The key is found in 2 Corinthians 5:15-17. These compelling words follow his declaration concerning the constraining power of love.

> *And that he died for all, that they which live should not hence-forth live unto themselves, but unto him which died for them, and rose again. Wherefore henceforth know we no man after the flesh: yea, though we have known Christ after the flesh, yet now henceforth know we him no more. Therefore if any man be in Christ, he is a new creature: old things are passed away; behold, all things are become new.*

When you realize that somebody died in your place—paid the ulti-mate sacrifice—your response to that truth will determine what you are willing to do with your own life. You begin to realize that it is not about you. It's not about what you think. It's not about your agenda. It's not about how you feel. It's not about if anybody loves you. When you love Him, when you honestly love Him with your heart, soul, mind, and strength, you are willing to do anything to advance His cause. When you honestly love Him, it moves you, doesn't it? The One who made the ultimate sacrifice enables you to make your sacri-fice. You understand that any sacrifice you make pales in comparison to His sacrifice.

C.T. Studd (1860-1931) is a member of the missionary hall of fame. He was a key member of the Cambridge cricket team—once the greatest team of all time. After hearing British Protestant missionary to Chin, a Hudson Taylor (1832-1905), speak, seven of the best members of that team (including Studd) left the team and went to China as missionaries. Can you imagine if that happened to some sports team today? It would be blasted all over the news. The commentators would dissect every facet of the news story. What would cause these seven guys to leave all this glory and go to China? It was the love of Christ.

While in China, Studd received news that he had become eligible to receive a large sum of money from an inheritance his father gave him. Much to the dismay of his family, he quickly proceeded to give 5000 British pounds to the ministry of American evangelist Dwight L. Moody (1837-1899), founder of the Moody Bible Institute. Then he gave 5000 pounds to the ministry of Christian evangelist and director of the Ashley Down orphanage in Bristol, England, George Muller (1805-1898). In the end, he gave away all of that inheritance to missions.

Suffering major physical issues and being rejected by every missionary society, Studd eventually left England for the Congo where he started the Worldwide Evangelization Crusade. He died at the age of 70 in his beloved Congo from untreated gallstones. His best-known statement contains these provoking words, *"If Jesus Christ be God and died for me, then no sacrifice can be too great for me to make for Him."*

The love that contains you will move you because you love Him, and you know that it's never enough. Many have gone before you. They have paid the price for the love they have for Christ and the world. They have been moved to uncomfortable places and some have given up their lives for the cause of Christ. For the love of Christ, others have moved into business, education, medical fields, and other places of service. There's a love that moves people into places of service that are inexplicable by normal understanding and human comprehension.

The love of Christ pushes you. The love of Christ restrains you. The love of Christ contains you. Once you have been introduced to the love of Christ, you will never be the same. You will see the world much differently than those around you. You will do things that others will call crazy. You will say things that confound people. As the earlier followers of Christ left everything to follow Him, the true followers of Jesus will abandon all for the love of God. Your love of Christ is defined and illustrated in what you are willing to do for Him. The others will never understand your actions, until they experience that great love for themselves. It is the only motivating force worth embracing and even dying for.

Chapter 7

Committed to a Cause: You Have to Go Through It to Get to It

"It is not the critic who counts: not the man who points out how the strong man stumbles or where the doer of deeds could have done better. The credit belongs to the man who is actually in the arena, whose face is marred by dust and sweat and blood, who strives valiantly; who errs and comes short again and again; because there is not effort without error and shortcomings; but who does actually strive to do the deed; who knows the great enthusiasms, the great devotions, who spends himself in a worthy cause; who, at the best, knows, in the end, the triumph of high achievement, and who, at the worst, if he fails, at least he fails while daring greatly, so that his place shall never be with those cold and timid souls who know neither victory nor defeat."[1]

very personal objective will be opposed by a potent obstacle. Anything worth achieving will meet resistance. It takes perseverance, wisdom, and faith to triumph over those opposing forces. As I have taught people around the world, you have to go through it to get to it. Life doesn't serve you a plate of success, without the personal ingredients necessary for that success. Along with those ingredients, believe me, you will be baked in the oven of opposition. Great leaders have constantly fought against the status quo and are tenacious in their efforts to create a breakthrough. We need a new generation of heroes that will rise up and take a city.

In 2 Samuel 5, we are introduced to a cadre of such champions in David's mighty army. The tribes of Israel had come to David while he was in Hebron and they had made him king. In that same Hebron, David ruled as king for over seven years. Toward the end of his reign in Hebron, David brought his army to the gates of Jerusalem with the purpose of making Jerusalem the capital of the Jewish kingdom.

There was only one rather huge problem confronting David. The Jebusites controlled that great walled city at that time and stood as an obstacle to David's objective of conquering Jerusalem. Taking Jerusalem would not be an easy task. On the west side of Jerusalem are the Judean Mountains and on the east side is the Judean desert that descends downward toward the Dead Sea. Jerusalem was built on four hills: Zion, Acra, Moriah and Bezetha. The hills were made of limestone with steep ascents on all sides. Each mountain was separated by valleys. Combined with the walls around the city, it made an assault virtually impossible.

Inside those walls were the Jebusites. Who were these Jebusites? They were believed to be descendants of Ham and lived in the mountain and hill areas of southern Israel. They were a fierce and defiant people that resisted being conquered by Israel. Jerusalem had been a neutral city until the Jebusites had taken control of it. One can sense that this great city was waiting for its coming king, the coming of David, who would bring national glory to that great city. These Jebusites were the only ones standing in David's way of accomplishing his dream.

A Tactic that Defies the Taunting

No great deed is ever easy; otherwise, everyone would do it. Extraordinary actions are reserved for remarkable people and heroes are born for moments like these.

> *And the king and his men went to Jerusalem unto the Jebusites,*
> *the inhabitants of the land: which spake unto David, saying,*
> *Except thou take away the blind and the lame, thou shalt not*
> *come in hither: thinking, David cannot come in hither.*
> —2 Samuel 5:6

From the top of the walls, the Jebusites were thrusting their taunting words in the direction of David's army. It reminds one of the verbal abuse from the mouth of Goliath. Days upon days he taunted the children of Israel until young David appeared and put an end to his devilish chatter. The Jebusites felt secure on top of the well-fortified city and told the soldiers below that even the blind and the lame could protect the city. In essence, they were saying that their city was so well

> Every successful person has discovered that the higher you go the more people there will be that will criticize you, taunt, and ridicule you.

fortified, so well protected that even the weakest among them could protect the city against their mighty army. Feeling safe in their citadel, they assumed that it would not take any effort to resist David and his mighty men.

Every successful person has discovered that the higher you go the more people there will be that will criticize you, taunt, and ridicule you. As someone has said, "Higher levels, bigger devils." Resistance is inevitable, and there will always be those naysayers sitting on the sidelines criticizing your every move.

As American essayist, lecturer and poet Ralph Waldo Emerson (1803-1882) said, *"Whatever you do you need courage. Whatever course you decide upon, there will always be someone to tell you that you are wrong. There are always difficulties arising that tempt you to believe your critics are right."*[2] Never listen to the critics that have, at no time, ever done anything. It is easy to sling mud, but harder to build something with that mud. It is easier to be an observer and much harder to be a participant.

The taunting of the Jebusites inspired David, rather than discouraging him. We read David's response in 2 Samuel 5:7-8—*Nevertheless David took the strong hold of Zion: the same is the city of David. And David said on that day, Whosoever getteth up to the gutter, and smiteth the Jebusites, and the lame and the blind that are hated of David's soul, he shall be chief and captain. Wherefore they said, The blind and the lame shall not come into the house.*

David gave them a choice. This could have been easy. They could have surrendered Jerusalem and David would have spared them, but they didn't. Bad idea! David let them know that because of their jesting, he would kill those very ones that they thought could easily protect them. David turned away from the heckling and looked at his men and offered them a challenge. Whoever goes up the gutter pipe, enters the city, and neutralizes the enemy, I will make them a chief and a captain.

Without going into too much detail, let me create a word picture of what this challenge required. The Jebusites occupied this fortified city, taunting David and his men. David and his men were situated on the southeastern corner of the great city. David presented the challenge that came with a reward. Everything sounded great, except that he had given them an impossible task. How were they going to get into the city? There was no way they could climb up the cliffs and then, somehow, scale up the walls and get into the city. It would be almost impossible and it would be a suicide mission.

At the bottom of that southeast corner is the Gihon Spring. In fact, the spring still exists to this day. The spring was an intermittent spring that was the only source of water for the whole city. Inside the city were pools that were filled from the water of that spring. An intricate system of tunnels and caves had been dug that spiraled downward inside the mountain and then outward to reach the Gihon Spring. The main tunnel plunged straight down about sixty feet through the interior of the mountain and then extended outward till it reached the outer wall. This intricate water system is called the "Warren's Shaft," named from the archaeologist who discovered it.

Most of us grew up being taught that it was through that ancient shaft that Joab and his men got into the city. However, we now know that this shaft was not created until 701 B.C. under Hezekiah. This event in 2 Samuel took place around 1000 B.C. That is almost a 300-year discrepancy. Kind of blows the whole theory, doesn't it?

We are still stuck with a dilemma. How did they get into the city? There was a piping system in those days, but it was not Warren's shaft. We get some insight by looking at the word used for *gutter*. This word *gutter* in the eighth verse is a very interesting word. The Hebrew word is *Tsinnor*. It is similar and related to the word *pipes* used in Zechariah 4:12, the word *Tsanteroth*. It is one of the words where we get the combination of our word "sanitation." Here is the revelation. This was a gutter pipe, in other words, a sewer pipe. It was the only way to get inside the city.

Now we have a clearer picture as to the challenge that these men faced. There was a pipe, actually there were several pipes that would descend down from the city, through the interior of the mountain and come out near the Gihon Spring. The inhabitants of the city used this pipe to dispose of their refuse. So David said, "Whoever leads the army into the city, whoever can figure out how to get in there, I will make you a leader. I will make you the captain in the army. But in order to do that, you're going have to go through the sewer to get there."

So, how do you really take a city for God? Is it possible? I think it is. But now you know why not very many people do it. Now you know why not many churches really go the extra mile to transform their city. To really penetrate and transform a city, you must endure the taunting and ridiculing of others. You are going to have to go through some tight places that are filled with refuse. You will get dirty. You will want to give up. This is only for the courageous of heart.

Finding an Opening

All success begins with an opening, an opportunity. When you start talking about taking a city, it is more difficult and more demanding than anyone thinks. I'm talking about making an impact, an impression, to penetrate, to get into something where you can do something from the inside out, rather from the outside in. To impact any people group, it is not enough to do this from the outside. It's not enough to throw rocks at it. Somewhere, you have to find an opening. You have to find an opportunity that will get you inside. All they needed was one opening. It takes a new set of eyes and a courageous disposition to see the opportunity. I like how British Prime Minister Winston Churchill (1874-1965) put it, *"A pessimist sees the difficulty in every opportunity; an optimist sees the opportunity in every difficulty."*

David's men were courageous optimists. They found the opening. It wasn't much of an opening, but it was an opening. There were about fifteen 24-inch sections of pipes. Two feet of width is not much, especially when it is half filled with all kinds of sewage. Imagine sticking your head into that opening in the pipe and trying to drag yourself forward on your stomach through all that sewer water. This is a feat that could make it on that reality show, "The Fear Factor." They will have to crawl through human waste, garbage, all kinds of revolting stuff.

Let's be clear. Taking a city is not for the faint of heart. There won't be anyone in the stands cheering you on. You will face all sorts of opposition. You will be confronted with some very disgusting stuff. Courage and commitment will be required of you in order to take a city.

Another thing in those pipes was the remains of sacrifices. When they would make sacrifices, the leftovers, whatever was washed out of the basins was normally thrown down those pipes. When that truth first hit me, it made perfect sense. You will crawl through the remains of sacrifices of people who have gone before you. Others have gone before you. Others have paid the price. Others have paved the way. Others have made great sacrifices so that you can go through the opening. If it wasn't for some of the old timers, you wouldn't be where you are today.

Those who have gone before you did not have the technological advantages that this generation has. Many died of diseases. Many were murdered or imprisoned. Most of them lived in poverty. In spite of all the disadvantages and trials, they were faithful in creating a better space for future generations. You will have to crawl through some broken dreams and some sacrificial remains of a generation that gave everything they had to make a way for you.

We talk about sacrifice in these days, but it is all relative. I don't believe that the sacrifices of our times can be compared to the sacrifices made by the past generations. We should be thankful to God for the price that they were willing to pay. Some planted the seed and others are now reaping.

I want to mention one other thing about the garbage in those pipes. In those sewer pipes were the remains of the crippled, the lame and blind and aborted babies. They were the outcasts of a society that had no love for the disabled among them. Today, we live in a different time. The disabled have their rights. In those days, they had no rights. In fact, more often than not, they were stoned or murdered and tossed into the sewer pipes. I have built this ministry and given my life to rescue such as these. If you want to take a city, you will have to do the same.

> It takes a special breed of men and women to take a city.

There are still some who have no rights, like the unborn. Abortionists have, literally, killed millions of unborn babies. I remember once when I was doing my bus route and saw a dog tearing apart one of the black garbage bags and eating something. At that time, I was out of my bus and was just walking by on visitation and happened to look over and that dog was eating a fetus. Somebody had thrown a dead fetus in the garbage. I am horrified by such disregard for human life. We still have our battles to fight.

It takes a special breed of men and women to take a city. Many go into the ministry with visions of grandeur, having no clue of the sacrifices that will be required of them. There is a price to be paid to go through any open door. *"Sacrifice is a part of life. It's supposed to be. It's not something to regret. It's something to aspire to."*[3] There will always be an opening, an opportunity, but the question is, "Are you willing to make the sacrifice to go through that opening?"

> Taking a city is not for the faint of heart. There won't be anyone in the stands cheering you on.

Free Up a Leader

Whenever an opening appears, a leader will arise. In order to take a city, it will require men and women of courage, conviction, and capability. Some leader has to be freed up to traverse the line into the land of opportunity. In looking at my own life and the life of other successful leaders, I have discovered that real leaders are filled with great passion. Some might interpret that passion as anger, and so it might be. Bahamian evangelist Myles Munroe (1954-) once said that whatever makes you angry is probably tied to your purpose. Not just anybody can go through an opening. It takes someone who has great passion. What are the things that you see around you that make you angry? Is it poverty, abortion, our educational system, addictions, or the number of divorces in America? Whatever it is just might be a clue to where God wants to take you.

I hate the injustice that exists in our world. My anger is the visible expression of my invisible passion. I know that because few will do what I do to fight the injustices of life that I must be the mouthpiece that speaks on behalf of those who cannot speak for themselves. I have seen what famine and disease have done to young children. It is always the children who pay the price for the sins of the adults. It infuriates me and forces me to do what is necessary to go through every opening made available to me.

Unfortunately, too many people have become disinterested in the conditions that exist in our world. They have overdosed on images of war and drought and hunger and disease and it has left them in a state of apathy. Where is the compassion of Christ? This generation is so concerned with their own needs that they have no time for the world around them. Romanian-born Jewish-American political activist Elie Wiesel (1928-), Holocaust survivor and writer, once said that the opposite of love is not anger, but indifference. How true! I have done what I can to awaken the sleeping giant and help the Church to see the needs that exist all around them. I am looking for a leader to take a city.

Second Chronicles 11:6 tells us that Joab was the first to climb through that opening and help take the city. Joab was committed to King David and willing to make himself vulnerable as he approached the opening. Joab and those who followed him had to take off all of their protective armor in order to squeeze into that narrow shaft. This sounds like a suicide mission, but they were the willing ones. They were willing enough to enter that pipe without any protection, overcome the panic created by claustrophobia, crawl through and endure all that sewage as they dragged themselves through for love of the king.

What crazy thing are you willing to do to take a city? Where is your courage? Where is your passion? How vulnerable are you willing to become? What are you willing to risk? Taking a city is not for the wimp and the wussy. It is not for the nervous Nellies or those that need to be coddled. It takes real men and women of character, hardened in the heat of battle, men and women of courage who know what it's like to be on the frontlines and will not retreat at the first sign of danger. Only these types of folk are eligible to go through an opening.

Your degrees and all your respectability won't protect you in the day of battle. There are no safe places for those who want to work for God. We are in a battle and only the strong will survive and finish the course.

Finish the Course

The hardest thing in life is to finish the course. We embrace an opportunity, we are willing to pay the price, but in the middle of the journey and when the goal still seems so far away, we are tempted to give up. The question haunts us. How far are you willing to go? I am sure that Joab and the men behind him were thinking the same thing. They never imagined how difficult it would be to crawl through this filthy pipe. They were at the halfway point, their muscles were cramping up, their mouths and noses were filled with sewage. However, there was no point in turning back. They couldn't, even if they wanted to. No way to turn around in such a limited space. There was only one choice: finish the course. Why would they quit when they had come so far?

> Success demands that you keep your eye on the prize.

When I was shot a few years ago, there were people who thought I would quit. It was a stupid thought on their part. How could I quit when I had already endured so much? Besides, what is there to go back to that is more valuable than what is ahead of us?

Life is not a sprint; it is a marathon that requires pacing, bravery, determination and endurance. Success demands that you keep your eye on the prize. American civil rights activist Rosa Parks (1913-2005) sat down so that the whole world could stand up. Because she refused to go to the back of the bus, she gave courage to thousands who boycotted the bus companies in Montgomery, Alabama. Their commitment to justice eventually led to the Supreme Court ruling against the bus companies' unjust law of discrimination.

"However, there will always be mountains to climb, valleys to tunnel through and rivers to cross, but never give up."[4]

You Got to Go Through It to Get to It

When these men finally inched their way out of that sewer hole, the task was not yet completed. They had to go through the sewage to get to the main battle, awaiting them in the streets of Jerusalem. When you finally get to the city, you have to fight. After you are exhausted, tired, stinking, not looking like you want another conflict. You don't smell like you want to fight. You don't feel like you want to engage your enemy.

There you are, standing at the edge of that dreaded hole you just climbed out of. The words of David are still ringing in their ears, ... *Whosoever smiteth the Jebusites first shall be chief and captain. So Joab the son of Zeruiah went first up, and was chief* (1 Chronicles 11:6).

Joab was the first to get into the hole, the first to emerge out of the pipes below, and he was the first to smite the Jebusites. Joab, a nephew of King David, was the same one who had killed Abner out of revenge. For that act, he got kicked out of David's army.

Because of his foolishness, lack of self-discipline, and lack of ability, he had failed. He was in this situation as the last opportunity to get back into the good graces of David. I can hear him thinking these words: *I have got one more chance to prove my worth to the king. I've been a screw-up to this point. I've messed up. I've made a lot of mistakes. I didn't do things well. I didn't produce. I have one last opportunity to show the king I can be trusted.* And without even hesitating, he jumped in the hole and crawled through the sewer water in the pipes, and without giving up he emerged from the pipe and smote the Jebusites. Because of this great feat, he was restored to his position as chief and captain of the armies of David.

How desperately do you want to succeed? I have discovered that inspiration and courage rises out of the fires of desperation. Our silent desperation must give way to noisy action. William Burroughs (1914-1997), the American novelist, once said that desperation is the raw material of drastic change. No great thing can ever be accomplished without the energy of desperation. However, the kind of desperation I am looking for is not an oppressive force that binds us to the past, but a fuel that drives us to success and restoration.

There is one last tidbit to this story. The Jebusites never thought that any of David's men would dare enter the city through those sewer pipes. Therefore they did not leave any sentry at the opening of the pipe into the city. Once Joab was outside the pipe, he did not kill the Jebusites. He just pushed them back into their little place, while his followers secured the city for David's entry.

All they did was just say, "Okay, now we're in charge. We're making the calls now. We're making the decisions. Shut up and go stay in your little hut. We are repossessing the city. We're not going kill you this time, but if you get stupid again, we may have to. So just go back to your little part over there—to your little place. You are now under a new rule. You're under a new law. You're under a new governance." The Jebusites were so brave at the top of the walls of the city, heckling the army of David. Now that Joab had broken through with his men, their courage evaporated into fear.

I don't know what you are going through, but if you are going to take a city for God, you will need to find an opening. When I came to New York many years ago, I found an opening. It was very painful. I've had to crawl through a lot of stuff. You will too. I am passionately angry at what I see around the world. I'm angry when I go out into townships in Africa and see the plight of so many children. I'm angry when I stand in a garbage dump knee deep and see the kids picking

> How bad do you want to take a city for God?

through the garbage in order to find something to eat. It angers me. I don't know what angers you. I don't know what makes you mad. I'm not talking about angry, because you were offended. That's foolish anger. I'm talking about being angry at the injustice and hopelessness of other people's conditions.

How much are you willing to go through? Are you willing to finish the course or will you retreat in fear? There had better be enough fire in you that once you have crawled through some rejection and ridicule and tough times, you can still do battle.

I know how tough life can be. I know how easy it can be to give up, even when victory is in sight. I know that a sucker punch by the enemy can take your breath away. However, that is the moment when you must stand strong.

In concluding this chapter, I leave you with this question. How bad do you want to take a city for God? Whatever you've crawled through in your past, whatever you're crawling through now, whatever you will crawl through in the future, somewhere in the middle of that pipe when you're all by yourself and feeling pity for yourself, remember there are people who have been through a whole lot more than you, and they came out the other side and fought to take a city, And they made a difference.

Scottish clergyman John Knox (1514-1572); Scottish landowner turned leader in the Wars of Scottish Independence, William Wallace (died 1305); Anglican cleric and Christian theologian John Wesley (1703-1791); the Moravian Church; Civil Rights leader Martin Luther King (1929-1968)—they all paid a great sacrifice to take a city. Now, it is your turn. What will you do to take a city? It all starts with finding an opening and crawling through it. It will demand endurance because you don't know how long that sewer pipe is. There will be moments of tears and jeers. There will be times when you don't think you will ever get through. Don't give up. Keep going forward. Even when you come out of those times, a battle awaits you. Do not be surprised how quickly the enemies will fall at your feet in those final moments. Somewhere there's an end to this thing. At some point you will be able to say with Paul that you have fought a good fight and you have finished the course.

Every time I go to Mexico, I experience that same anger. There have been so many missionaries down there that they should have been able to rebuild the whole country. It's still a mess. Drug dealers are willing to build tunnels for ten, fifteen miles underground from Mexico to come up into California, Arizona, and Texas. They have no problem crawling through those tunnels because they are desperate to make a buck.

Others are trying to crawl through to come to a place of freedom and safety. Look at what they have endured to get to our land of freedom. If they are willing to sacrifice everything, even death, why won't we do the same?

I don't know what will motivate you to crawl through a pipe, to edge through a tunnel. I don't know what it will take to make you wake up and do something. Maybe, once you get to a place of desperation, you will act. I hope you will.

When you want something badly enough, the fire of desperation will inspire you to change the world around you. Everything in our culture will fight against you. The self-centered spirit of this age will seek to sabotage the plans God has for you to take a city. You will have to fight it and overcome it. It is imperative that you discover a cause greater, something outside the circle of your own self interests. We are all in this together and NOW is the time to act and change a city.

Chapter 8

The Art of Effective Mentoring: The Demands of Dothan

"The mediocre teacher tells. The good teacher explains. The superior teacher demonstrates. The great teacher inspires."[1]

A well-known Buddhist proverb declares that when the student is ready, the teacher will appear. Teacher, mentor or coach, whatever you want to call it, is a key to affecting change in others. Samuel had an Eli. Joshua had a Moses. Elisha had an Elijah. Jesus chose twelve men to be His disciples. Timothy was mentored by Paul. One of the key moments in any person's life is the advent of the one that comes alongside to be their teacher.

This mentoring process is dependent upon two key factors: the readiness and openness of the student, combined with the experience and knowledge of the teacher. Until the apprentice is at a teachable place, there is no need for the master. Unless a mentor has gone through his own teaching process, gathering knowledge and experience along the way, he is not equipped to teach others. Before you can teach, you must be taught. The teachable moment happens when the master and disciple converge at the appropriate moment.

In 2 Kings 6 we get a glimpse into such a teachable moment. In order to understand the moment, we have to consider the context that triggered the moment.

Benhadad was king of Syria (or Aram as it is called in this passage). There were actually three kings of Syria with this name. It was Benhadad II that was king of Syria during the time of Elisha. Benhadad was a thorn in the side of Israel throughout his reign. Ahab, king of Israel (the northern kingdom) had a cantankerous relationship with Benhadad. Long wars with Israel characterized his reign. After the death of Ahab, Benhadad reinstated the war with Israel and attacked Samaria a second time.

> *Then the king of Syria warred against Israel, and took counsel with his servants, saying, In such and such a place shall be my camp. And the man of God sent unto the king of Israel, saying, Beware that thou pass not such a place; for thither the Syrians are come down. And the king of Israel sent to the place which the man of God told him and warned him of, and saved himself there, not once nor twice. Therefore the heart of the king of Syria was sore troubled for this thing; and he called his servants, and said unto them, Will ye not shew me which of us is for the king of Israel? And one of his servants said, None, my lord, O king: but Elisha, the prophet that is in Israel, telleth the king of Israel the*

words that thou speakest in thy bedchamber. And he said, Go and spy where he is, that I may send and fetch him. And it was told him, saying, Behold, he is in Dothan. Therefore sent he thither horses, and chariots, and a great host: and they came by night, and compassed the city about..

—2 Kings 6:8-14

Elisha was Benhadad's nemesis. In this chapter, we get a little insight into the adversarial relationship between the two. After the death of King Ahab, Benhadad decided to invade Israel again and had set a trap for Israel. Elisha warned King Jehoram, Ahab's son and the new King of Israel, about this Syrian snare and told him to avoid the area where the ambush was prepared. This happened over and over and caused Benhadab to become infuriated and a bit paranoid. He was suspicious of everyone. How was Israel aware of his every move? He was positive that there was a spy in his camp. The king's blood was boiling, convinced that someone in his camp was a traitor. Committed to finding out who from his entourage was warning Jehoram, he started asking his servants who was the betraying scoundrel in his camp. One of the servants assured him that there was no traitor. He went on to say that this was the work of Elisha the prophet and that he was the one revealing their secret plans to Jehoram. On hearing this news, Benhadab sent an army to Dothan to kidnap the prophet and put an end to his exasperating enablement of the King of Israel.

Now, Dothan is about 11 miles outside of Samaria. It is the same Dothan mentioned in Genesis 37:17 where Joseph found his brothers and where they put him in a well and eventually sold him into slavery. Elisha had made his residence in this ancient city.

When the servant of the man of God was risen early, and gone forth, behold, an host compassed the city both with horses and chariots. And his servant said unto him, Alas, my master! How shall we do? And he answered, Fear not: for they that be with us are more than they that be with them. And Elisha prayed, and said, LORD, I pray thee, open his eyes, that he may see. And the LORD opened the eyes of the young man; and he saw: and, behold, the mountain was full of horses and chariots of fire round about Elisha. And when they came down to him, Elisha prayed unto the LORD, and said, Smite this people, I pray thee, with blindness. And he smote them with blindness according to the word of Elisha. And Elisha said unto them, This is not the way, neither is this the city: follow me, and I will bring you to the man whom ye seek. But he led them to Samaria.

—2 Kings 6:15-20

Who Are You?

Elisha had been mentored by Elijah and because of that relationship he had a clear view of who he was. Elisha was prepared to take the first step to help his servant come into a clear vision of who he was. What determines who we are? There are many paths we could take to answer that question. There are many causes that go into our continuing development. We know that personality, environment, education and experiences are all contributing factors to where we start and what we become.

There are those who believe the starting place is determined by your personality. Understanding your personality traits can be helpful, but I want to say that it is not the only test for discovering who we are. The advocates of personality testing tell us that there are four major personality groups: choleric, sanguine, phlegmatic, and melancholic. When the denomination I used to be a part of thought I was having a nervous breakdown, they sent me to have all of these personality tests. These tests might be helpful for figuring out one part of the "'who you are" puzzle, but let me emphasize one more time that they are only one view of a complex issue.

Let me give you a quick overview on the four personalities or temperaments, as they are also called. The present-day view of the temperaments is not an original psychological view of human personality. It goes all the way back to Greek philosophers and doctors. "In 340 B.C. Plato wrote of four temperament types, which he called Artisan, Guardian, Idealist and Rational. In 325 B.C. Aristotle wrote of Hedonic, Proprietary, Ethical and Dialectical. In 190 A.D. Galen spoke of Sanguine, Melancholic, Choleric and Phlegmatic temperaments, which were based on the ideas of Hippocrates from as far back as 450 B.C."[2]

Teachers of the temperament tell us that all of us fall into one of these main groupings. However, they will say that these are not absolutes and that no one is a pure temperament type. The sanguine is very sociable, outgoing, and charismatic. They are people-oriented, enjoy making friends, optimistic and of a warm heart. The choleric is ambitious, task-oriented, makes a great leader and is very passionate. Because they are so task-oriented, they can dominate others and are often misunderstood. The phlegmatic is relaxed, non-confrontational, and loyal. They are given to resolving personal conflicts between others, prefer thinking and observing to getting involved, and they are consistent. The melancholic is introverted, creative, cautious, and they internalize everything. They are task-oriented and more loners than life of the party types.

Three Types of Man

As helpful as these designations might be, they are not as beneficial as understanding the three types of people that the Bible talks about. All of us have grown up putting people into classes. Academically, we speak of the educated and uneducated. Economically, we speak of the rich and poor. Culturally, we speak of upper class and lower class. Spiritually, the Bible talks about three classes of people. Once you begin to understand these types, you will start to realize how maturity is attained. These three Pauline descriptions of man give us insight into how we view ourselves and how we relate to God and man. Every one of us can be situated into one of these categories. Paul describes these three manners of man as natural, spiritual or carnal.

The Bible tells us that man was created as spirit, soul and body. We are spirit, have a soul, and live in a body. If we keep this order of man into proper relationship, we can live life successfully. If anything, other than the spirit, rises to dominance, our life will be out of balance.

The natural man is dead because it is detached from the spirit. The entrance of sin into the world killed the spirit of man. The light of God has been turned off, and he is not able to connect with God. In 1 Corinthians 2:14 Paul writes this description of the natural man, *But the natural man receiveth not the things of the Spirit of God: for they are foolishness unto him: neither can he know them, because they are spiritually discerned.*

He is ignorant of the Spirit and the life He offers to us. It's impossible to teach spiritual things to unspiritual people. Unspiritual people just don't get it. It's something like trying to teach a pig how to sing. Unspiritual people are devoid of spiritual reality. Even though there is a spiritual reality all around them, they are blinded to that reality. Unless the Spirit of God quickens it to them, unless somehow the Spirit of God draws them, they will remain in that darkened state.

The day Adam ate of the tree of the knowledge of good and evil, the light went out. He died, spiritually. It was on that day that man disconnected from God. Adam, as a representative of unspiritual man, was no longer getting the input from the Spirit of God. He fell into a state of the natural man. When you are disconnected, you cease to receive impulses from the Spirit of God. No longer do we get our motivation, or instruction, or direction, or guidance from a higher realm.

The natural man is a sense-driven person. He gets all of his information from the exterior senses such as sight, smell, hearing, taste, and touch. It is from the sense world, rather than the spirit world, that he gets his impulses and information. He is like the existential man that says, "Whatever turns you on, do it." The natural man does not acknowledge, appreciate, or apprehend the things of God.

The **spiritual man**, as described by Paul, lives through the Spirit. He has his origin of life from the Spirit. He depends upon the Spirit, rather than the flesh and its senses. He is crucified to the flesh, walks in the spirit, is alive in Christ, gets his input from the Word and does not take impulses from the flesh.

> *That the righteousness of the law might be fulfilled in us, who walk not after the flesh, but after the Spirit. … But to be spiritually minded is life and peace. But ye are not in the flesh, but in the Spirit, if so be that the Spirit of God dwell in you.*
>
> —Romans 8:4, 6a, 9

The spiritual man communes with God and is sensitive to His every word and impression. He seeks His guidance from the Spirit, rather than the soul. The man of the Spirit is guided by faith, rather than fear and its senses. He has submitted his mind, will and emotions to the Holy Spirit. All he does is in coordination with the Spirit. *Walking after the Spirit involves both the initiation of a work by revelation and executing it through the Lord's strength.*[3]

The **carnal man** is the description of too many Christians. He lives sandwiched between the flesh and the spirit and is a double-minded person. He is more concerned about how he feels and what he wants. Carnality quenches the spirit and is more inclined toward the soul, as opposed to the Spirit. The pathway to maturity is thwarted because the carnal man chooses to remain in his selfish condition.

> *For they that are after the flesh do mind the things of the flesh;*
> *but they that are after the Spirit the things of the Spirit.*
> —Romans 8:5

Too many people think that the answer is found at the altar. They don't understand that spiritual growth is a process, not a particular event. This is a battle for the mind. Many are praying to God to change things, when they should be praying for God to change them. That is the beginning point. The word *carnal* comes from that word where we get the word *carnivorous*, "the flesh, flesh eating, and impulses from the flesh." The carnal man is getting impulses from both directions, spirit and flesh. Therein, lies the conflict. Technically you can't be carnal, unless you're saved. The carnal man has experienced the life of the Spirit but he keeps fluctuating back and forth between the spiritual man and the carnal man. Paul calls it a war, a battle between spirit and flesh. You can be walking in the Spirit one minute and the next minute you can be as carnal as the natural man. So, we're caught in the middle, trying to please God while trying to please ourselves. It doesn't work!

Carnality is not drugs, alcohol, having affairs, doing all that stuff. You can be free from all of those addictions and still be carnal.

Galatians 5:19-21 says that some of the works of the flesh are lust, uncleanness, idolatry, witchcraft and heresy, but it also includes anger, envy, and strife. The carnal person has destroyed many churches and ministries by their gossiping and subversive actions. *For to be carnally minded is death; but to be spiritually minded is life and peace. Because the carnal mind is enmity against God: for it is not subject to the law of God, neither indeed can be. So then they that are in the flesh cannot please God* (Romans 8:6-8).

The carnal mind submits to the law of self, as opposed to the law of God. It cannot find peace because it lives in the crevice of the angst that exists between serving self and loving God. The eyes of the carnal man are blinded by his circumstances. As long as your focus is on your circumstances, you will never make it. If you allow them to, circumstances will overwhelm you. You will never be subject to the law of God. You will never be a person of faith.

> God did not create robots. He created human beings with a mind and will that can think and act freely.

We have made life so spiritual that we have put the whole thing on God. In other words, God is in control of everything, and we have no part in directing life's course. I grew up like that. We'd put it all on God. If God wants me to do something, He will make it happen. This is faulty thinking. God did not create robots. He created human beings with a mind and will that can think and act freely. Life is about YOU making choices. Does God intervene in our lives from time to time? Absolutely! But for the most part, our lives revolve around making accurate and strategic choices that reflect our commitment to God's purposes.

Another issue I have recognized is that a lot of people blame the devil for every wrong that happens in their lives or in the lives of the people around them. I have heard people say, "The devil has a hold of my wife!" "The devil has a hold on my husband." Are you kidding? I mean no disrespect, but the devil doesn't want your spouse. What's he going to do with him? He's got bigger problems. He doesn't need your wife or your husband. But he will attack what you care about. He will come at what is important to you in order to get to your mind. He attacks the things that he knows will distract and intimidate you so that he can mislead, confuse and distract you. The carnal mind falls into the devil's devices.

You don't need to rebuke the devil. You need to get a grip on your mind! I know what it's like to be the spiritual man, and I know what it's like to be the carnal man, because I've been both. Natural man has no options. He has no impulses from the Spirit. But the spiritual man has choices and the choices he makes determines if he shape shifts from spirituality to carnality.

It's easy to be a spiritual person when you live in a controlled and safe environment. If you could live your whole life in church, wouldn't life be better? I think we all know that it isn't possible. Don't get me wrong. The controlled environment of being with other believers is a good place. It is a place where we are refreshed and reinforced for life outside the church. It is on the outside where life is tested and made resilient.

Get Up and Go Through

And when the servant of the man of God was risen early, and gone forth, behold, an host compassed the city both with horses

*and chariots. And his servant said unto him, Alas, my master!
How shall we do?*

—2 Kings 6:15

The young man in this story got up early. Getting up places you in a new level of opportunity and vision. The higher we go, the higher the risks. I have noticed that most Christians hate change. The space below that new level is a sanctuary of safety. When you get up and go up, you are faced with a new collection of choices. When God moves you to the next level, all of a sudden, you're going to be dealing with stuff you have never dealt with before.

You're fighting things you never fought before. The initial excitement of rising to another status will begin to wane, when it dawns upon us that this new place brings more responsibility, challenges and predicaments.

The young man got up, went outside expecting that this day would be like any other day. To his surprise he saw the Syrian army surrounding the city. Let me just say this. You can't win without a conflict. The Bible says that I'm more than a conqueror, but how can you be a conqueror, unless there's a fight? Trouble only confronts people that are effective. When you get up to a new level, it will require that you go through something.

The apostle Peter, a man who knew a lot of trouble, wrote these words, *Beloved, think it not strange concerning the fiery trial which is to try you, as though some strange thing happened unto you* (1 Peter 4:12). Persecution, resistance, and opposition should not be a peculiar enigma to the ones who are called to live in the high places. In John 16:33 Jesus told His disciples that in this world we will have tribulation. Why are we shocked when we are confronted with a conflict?

There have been times in my life that I was almost sure that this was it. I'm not going to make it. I can't pull through this. But I can look back at every success I have achieved and realize that I achieved it because I chose to ignore the circumstances. People know what I have done, but they don't know what I have had to go through. I have fought my share of battles but I have learned that you don't have to live your life *under the circumstances*. You have to learn to live *above the circumstances*. I don't allow my life to be consumed by what my eyes see.

Nobody Knows the Trouble I See

The young man went outside his tent, and he looked around and freaked out by what he saw—the Syrian army. He thinks, *We're in trouble.* The impulses of the soul take control. *We're going to die here.* Even though he's been around the man of God and even though he's seen the miracles, he has still not learned the lesson. The spiritual man sees life with a new set of eyes.

Elisha, the mentor, saw what this young man did not see. Why was Elisha able to see what the young man could not see? Here's one way to look at it. Let's do a word play. Mentor is a man who is *touring*. How many times have we heard about a man that did three *tours* in Iraq? This man is not a newbie. He is not like the young man that just got out of boot camp. There is a whole world of difference. The veteran soldier has had training, mentoring, and experiences that the young recruit has not experienced. Life in the classroom is not enough. Maturity comes in the field. The only way to get that experience is to go through it. The experienced or seasoned warrior sees life through a different set of eyes.

This is the first lesson for this new student. You have to have a new pair of eyes in order to survive in this life. The only way to get those eyes is to go through some wars, to face the enemy, to see the power of God and to overcome. I don't trust those who have never been in the battle. There is something special about the wisdom of the seasoned saint. It's getting around somebody who has already stared into the eyes of the enemy and experienced victory on the battlefields of life. That's what mentoring is: It's the mentoring process.

Don't tell me how much faith you have, until you tell me how much fire you have been through. Spirituality is not how about how many gifts you have and how well you can preach. Spirituality is about overcoming, resisting and transcending. The best teacher is the one who has learned wisdom in the fire, through the storm and in the battle. I want to hang out with those who wanted to quit, who thought they were going to lose their mind, who have been betrayed and attacked, have been misunderstood, made mistakes and, through it all, have stood strong and prevailed in times of pain and pressure. That person can be my teacher any day.

Elisha was well trained, wasn't he? He had walked alongside his mentor, Elijah. First Kings 19:19 says that Elijah went out to the field and found Elisha. This is the first lesson in mentoring. The mentor chooses his student. The student does not choose the mentor. This was a divine connection. Elijah had been prepared to be an effective mentor. During times of apostasy and idolatry, Elijah was the lone voice speaking out against false gods and seeking to draw Israel back to Jehovah. He stood in the face of the evil King Ahab and caused God's judgment to fall upon those that rejected God. In many ways, Elijah prepared a path for Elisha. Elijah's relationship with Elisha was very unique and special. Elijah knew that a time would come when he would be taken. Elijah taught while Elisha watched, listened and observed. The moment came when the mentoring process was over. Elijah was taken and Elisha took up his friend's mantle. The God of Elijah was now his God.

Elisha's first lesson for the young man was that he needed to see life from God's perspective, in contrast to a distorted view from the soul. The Bible talks about trouble coming. Did you ever notice that the Bible never talks about help coming? The Bible never says that. That has always bothered me. The Bible always says trouble's coming, trouble's coming. Do you know why? Because already there. He's an ever present help in the time of trouble. When trouble arises, God is not surprised. He is already there to be a constant help in time of turmoil.

A Mentor's Prayer

And Elisha prayed, and said, LORD, I pray thee, open his eyes, that he may see. And the LORD opened the eyes of the young man; and he saw: and, behold, the mountain was full of horses and chariots of fire round about Elisha.

—2 Kings 6:17

Elisha realized that the young man was looking in a horizontal direction rather than a vertical one. The direction you are looking will determine the success that you will have. It's like flying in a plane. You see things that the ones below do not see. From the vantage point of the plane you can see the breaking clouds on the horizon, while those below live in the storm. We have done more here in New York with the worst facilities imaginable and that's the beauty of this ministry. I am sure that people come here thinking they will see some elaborate, expensive facilities. I am just as sure that they all just shake their head and think *how in the name of anything that's intelligent can these people be doing what they're doing with as little as they have?* That's the wonder of what we do. Because it's not us. What they don't see is that I don't invest in buildings; I'm investing in people. I wish other ministries understood this powerful truth.

Elisha prayed that God would open his eyes. He didn't preach at him—he prayed for him. Robert Frost's words ring true here. "I am not a teacher. I am an awakener."[4] With his prayer, Elisha awakened the young student and helped him to see what he saw.

When his eyes opened, his mouth was left agape. He was seeing something he never saw before. The best way he could describe what he saw was *chariots of fire.*

> **God has weapons for your protection that you have never imagined.**

The Syrians' chariots were wooden chariots and would not survive a fire. The weapons of God have been tested by fire. They are more powerful than the weapons of your enemies. God has weapons for your protection that you have never imagined. He has some stuff to fight on your behalf that you never thought of.

The angels of God were there, but they weren't there to fight. They were there to comfort. At times God will open your eyes to see into His world and that heavenly vision will encourage you and assist you to live in your world. It changes your perspective, doesn't it?

Mentors Teach by Example

And when they came down to him, Elisha prayed unto the LORD, and said, Smite this people, I pray thee, with blindness. And he smote them with blindness according to the word of Elisha. And Elisha said unto them, This is not the way, neither is this the city: follow me, and I will bring you to the man whom ye seek. But he led them to Samaria. And it came to pass, when they were come into Samaria, that Elisha said, LORD, open the eyes of these men, that they may see. And the LORD opened their eyes, and they saw; and, behold, they were in the midst of Samaria. And the king of Israel said unto Elisha, when he saw them, My father, shall I smite them? shall I smite them? And he answered, Thou shalt not smite them: wouldest thou smite those whom thou hast taken captive with thy sword and with thy bow? set bread and water before them, that they may eat and drink, and go to their master. And he prepared great provision for them: and when they had eaten and drunk, he sent them away, and they went to their master. So the bands of Syria came no more into the land of Israel.

—2 Kings 6:18-23

What happened? Elisha prayed that the Lord would blind the eyes of the Syrians. Actually, the word for *blindness* is the Hebrew word *sanverim*. The only other time this unique word is used is in Genesis 19:11, where the angels in Lot's house smote the men of Sodom with a blindness. "*Modern research has called our attention between the word 'Sanverim' and the Akkandain word 'Shunuvurum' that translates as having extraordinary brightness.*"[5] They were not blinded by a shadowy darkness, but by a dazzling light. Their mental faculties were confused so that they would see things that weren't there and not see things that were there. They could see, but could not realize what they were seeing. It was confusing.

Now, we enter into an interesting part of the story. Looking at the Syrian forces, in their confused sight, Elisha said, "I'm not the guy. This is not the right city, but I'll take you to the guy and the right city." Sometimes, a little lie is okay. Elisha brought them right into the middle of Samaria, and the king asked if he could kill them. What did Elisha say, "Nope, don't kill them. Feed them." What? That makes no sense.

> The spiritual man asks God to give him strength to go through the trouble, rather than delivering him from trouble.

Feed them. So what was the point of this whole story? I read this about 20 times trying to figure out the meaning of this event. At first, I thought this was dumb. *Just kill them.* Here is the lesson. God is more concerned about what you learn from your enemies than killing your enemies. The spiritual man asks God to give him strength to go through the trouble, rather than delivering him from trouble.

The story ends with Elisha going back to Dothan and the Syrians going back to their city and they never attacked Israel again. Everything was the same except one thing, the student's mentality. Everything else was the same, except one man learned a lesson that was etched into his spirit. He would never look at life the same. This was the day that the student got the lesson and that lesson would last for a life-time. He saw something he had never seen before. He opened his eyes, and God allowed him to see something that would teach him to never trust his senses, but to trust the Spirit. That is a great lesson that we must all learn.

So what are the demands of Dothan? Once you've seen the power of God, you are responsible for what you have seen. You will be held accountable, my friend. For what you see and what you understand and what you learn and how you walk, you will be held accountable. It's not about anybody else. It's not about what they do or what they do not do. It's about the day that your eyes are opened to see. Associate Justice of the U.S. Supreme Court Oliver Wendell Holmes, Jr. (1841-1935) wrote these poignant words, "Once the mind has been stretched by a new idea, it will never again return to its original size."[6] Once you have seen something and once you have learned something, you will never be the same. You are now responsible for the insight that came from the experience. You can't go back and say I did not know. You are responsible for the truth revealed to you. Hold it tight and never let it go.

That is the lesson from Dothan. May you learn it well!

Chapter 9

Proven Warrior: If You Don't Put Them Up, You Can't Take Them Down

"Experience is not what happens to a man; it is what a man does with what happens to him." [1]

There is a Norwegian proverb that says experience is a good teacher but the tuition is high. Education has changed a lot in this generation. There was a time in the history of our nation when many people were trained under a master. The apprentice would be taught the art of a trade through a master that taught using the method of "show and tell." They learned in the field rather than the classroom. Today, students are taught by professors who have never had any experience in the field. Learning in the lab of a classroom is much different than learning in the workshop of the world. Experience is a hard way to learn because you get the test first and the answers afterward, but what a way to learn.

To emphasize this truth, I will tell you a story. We start with the story of King Jehoram, the same king who Elisha helped against the Syrian army. Jehoram married Athaliah and a bad marriage it was. Jehoram did his best to promote the worship of Yahweh, while his wicked wife promoted the worship of Baal.

After Jehoram died, her son Ahaziah, became king and Athaliah became his official advisor. While on a state visit to the Northern Kingdom, Ahaziah was killed and died at Megiddo, leaving an open door for the Queen. Athaliah, the wicked mother, came in and took over the throne. Her first treacherous act was to kill all of her grandchildren, all the boys that would be legal heirs to the throne. Jehosheba, the sister of Athaliah, stole the last little boy, Jehoash, and raised him for seven years in the house of the Lord.

Bring Back the King

Jehosheba's husband, the high priest, Jehoiada, entered the story when the boy was seven years old and was now technically old enough to become the king. The drama in this story leads up to 2 Kings 11. They were ready to bring the boy out of hiding—ready to put him on the throne. Jehoiada knew that Athaliah would not go out easily. She was ready to put up a fight to protect her throne. Jehoida had a shrewdly-shaped plan to bring down Athaliah and replace her with Joash as the king.

And the seventh year Jehoiada sent and fetched the rulers over hundreds, with the captains and the guard, and brought them to

him into the house of the LORD, and made a covenant with them,
and took an oath of them in the house of the LORD, and shewed
them the king's son. And he commanded them, saying, This is
the thing that ye shall do; A third part of you that enter in on
the sabbath shall even be keepers of the watch of the king's house;
and a third part shall be at the gate of Sur; and a third part at
the gate behind the guard: so shall ye keep the watch of the house,
that it be not broken down. And two parts of all you that go forth
on the sabbath, even they shall keep the watch of the house of the
LORD about the king.

—2 Kings 11:4-7

The New American Standard version of verse 4, along with other translations, translates the ancient text with these words, *Now in the seventh year Jehoiada sent and brought the captains of hundreds of the Carites and of the guard…* The Orthodox Jewish Bible renders the translation in this fashion, *And the seventh year Yehoyada sent and got the commanders of hundreds, with the Kereti…* Who were the Carites? There is some speculation that the Carites were the same as the Cherethite mentioned in various passages in the times of David. In 2 Samuel 15:18 they are listed as part of David's army that fought against Absalom. The Abingdon Old Testament Commentary has this to say about the Carites, "*Though the Carites' origin and identity is uncertain, they were most likely an elite group, perhaps a cadre, of influential mercenaries.*"[2] As possible descendants of the Cherethites, those special forces were committed to preserving and restoring the Davidic line to the throne, usurped by Athaliah.

Jehoiada orchestrated a plan to dethrone the queen and place the child king on the throne, thus restoring the Davidic royal lineage. First, he brought the elite guard to the Temple and made a covenant with them, assuring their commitment to his plan. Then, he brought forth Jehoash before this band of warriors. You can imagine their surprise. They, no doubt, thought that the whole lineage of David had been murdered. I am sure this only heightened their pledge to Jehoiada's plan. The Sabbath was the chosen day to put the plan into effect. Finally, Jehoiada organized the strategic placement of the troops. The passage is a little confusing, but we can easily assume that he placed a third of the soldiers around the Temple to protect the young king, and the others were sectioned off to cover the duties around the palace and the Temple, in preparation for the final assault on Athaliah.

Showcase of Success

And ye shall compass the king round about, every man with his weapons in his hand: and he that cometh within the ranges, let him be slain: and be ye with the king as he goeth out and as he cometh in. And the captains over the hundreds did according to all things that Jehoiada the priest commanded: and they took every man his men that were to come in on the sabbath, with them that should go out on the sabbath, and came to Jehoiada the priest. And to the captains over hundreds did the priest give king David's spears and shields, that were in the Temple of the LORD. *And the guards stood, every man with his weapons in his hand, round about the king, from the right corner of the Temple to the left corner of the Temple, along by the altar and the Temple.*

—2 Kings 11:8-11

The priest had prepared the soldiers to guard the little boy king, as Joash was introduced to the people. Jehoiada was very wise. He was going to make the transition on the Sabbath, because there could not be a lot of coming and going on the Sabbath. So, the first shift of guards would still be there and the second shift would be ready to take their place. By doing it this way, he was maximizing his chances for success. There was one last thing to do and that was to equip the soldiers with weapons.

Now, we get to an interesting part of the story. Verse 10 says that the captains over hundreds came to the priest, and he gave them weapons to be used in defense of the king and to bring down the followers of Athaliah. These weapons were located in the Temple and they were the ancient weapons of King David. Josephus, the Jewish historian, wrote about David's armory in his book of Antiquities. *"Josephus expressly says that David had provided an arsenal for the Temple, out of which Jehoiada too took those arms. And Jehoiada having opened the arsenal in the Temple, which David had prepared, he divided among the centurions, priests, and Levites, the spears, arrows, and quivers, and all other kinds of weapons which he found there."*[3]

We don't have much information on this armory of weapons, but we do know that David saved some of the weapons from his battles, either his own favorite weapons used in battle, or the choice weapons of his enemies that he took from the battlefield. He gathered these weapons, after the battle was over, brought them to the Temple, and stored them there as a document to his victories. They were hung on a wall in a room that was sort of a museum. Evidently, there were some weapons that were used in battle that had a certain significance above just the normal shield, the normal sword, the normal spear. They became a showcase of his victories.

Why did he create this room? Certainly, it would be a testimony to future generations of their past victories, but I think that he put them there for future use by those generations. This was that day. The future of God's people was now on the line. If they were not able to win this battle against Athaliah and her loyal people, that would have been the end of the whole Davidic line. The future of Jehovah's people was at stake.

David chose to take the weapons that he had used, that he had proved and preserve them for another generation. Every great leader, I believe, has a desire to leave something behind for the next generation. David knew that he would not live forever, so he left something that could provide protection and support for those in the future. That desire to leave something for the next generation should be a passion of every generation. Without generational thinking, the future is at risk. This is why I am writing this book and the other books I have written. I am leaving a testimony of truth for the next generation. My books are my witness, my story and the things I have learned that will encourage and inspire future generations. They are a part of my legacy for the generations to come.

However, those weapons hanging on the wall, every weapon of warfare that was hung on that wall, all the remnants of his life, were all the vestiges of a life that was lived fighting battles for Jehovah. There was more to it than just a bunch of museum pieces, more than just a bunch of artifacts that were hung up on a wall. Here is the central point of this chapter: if you don't hang'em up, you can never pull'em down. If David hadn't put these weapons up, no one could take them down. They were in reserve for this momentous time in history. Verse 11 says that the guards stood, every one of them, with a weapon in their hands, and verse 10 makes it clear that these weapons were not for the ordinary soldier. They were preserved for the experienced warriors, the elite guard that were leaders of men.

They knew the history. They knew the background. Probably, most of them were descendants of David's mighty army. They were committed to maintaining the royal line of David. They had their experience in battle and knew the taste of victory. Jehoiada would never put these weapons in the hands of a novice.

We understand why David put these weapons in the room, now we will look at the individual weapons and what they mean to us. I want to take a walk through that room. I want to take you on a little tour of the museum and look at each weapon of war.

Slingshot of Single-Mindedness

The slingshot was David's first weapon, and he used it mightily. It's a slingshot from Bethlehem. This isn't just any slingshot—it's special. Over in 1 Samuel 17:40 we read, *And he took his staff in his hand, and chose him five smooth stones out of the brook, and put them in a shepherd's bag which he had, even in a scrip; and his sling was in his hand: and he drew near to the Philistine.* This was the same sling that he used back in Bethlehem to kill the bear and the lion.

But, what kind of a slingshot is it? I believe it's the slingshot of single mindedness. He was smart enough to know that, even in his youth, even as a young boy, he was being prepared for something that he didn't even understand. He didn't know where his life was going then. But God had a plan for him. God was preparing him for a much greater event. He got his training in the wilderness and the day he met Goliath, he was prepared to bring down the giant.

There are principles that we learn early in life that prepare us for bigger battles. I believe that I have been used to *ruin* peoples' lives. In other words, I have destroyed their illusions concerning ministry. I have helped them to see that it is not all glory. You had better be prepared to fight some tough battles if you are going to survive.

David was smart enough to know that, even as a boy, he had better be single minded. I could not have survived in this city, if I had not been prepared. Nobody knows the troubles I have seen. Nobody knows the private and public wars I have fought. I have endured because of the training I had as a young man.

David knew that even in his young age God was preparing him. The slingshot that he used to kill the lion, the slingshot that he used to kill the bear, would prepare him to kill a giant. Through it all, he was laying the foundation. It's a slingshot of single mindedness, of concentrated effort to succeed in all that he did.

Staff of Remembrance

There was a staff hanging on that wall. Why a staff? That is no weapon. First Samuel 17:40 says that with his staff in his hand he picked up the five stones that would be used in his sling to kill Goliath. Goliath saw David coming in his direction and said, *And the Philistine said unto David, Am I a dog, that thou comest to me with staves? And the Philistine cursed David by his gods* (1 Samuel 17:43). Other translations call the staves *sticks*. Well, this was not just any staff. This was the staff of Eli who had anointed him to be king of Israel.

David was entering the next stage of his life. Follow me, now. Each weapon in the armory was part of the story of David's life. He was now going up a level. He was leaving the private life and entering the public stage. New levels bring bigger devils. Every stage of your life will bring new enemies to be conquered. This was the battle of a life-time. This would be the fight that would define him and launch him into his future.

Here is an important truth that you must grasp, if you are to be successful. Your battles define you and determine how high you will go up the ladder of success. Every situation in life has a significance attached to it. The key is to remain consistent in all that we do. It's taken me thirty-five years to become an overnight success. You cannot survive the public place if you have not been faithful in the private place. Survival requires consistency.

> It's what you have done consistently that matters.

It's not the one thing you have done in your life time that matters. It's what you have done consistently that matters. The repetition and practice of the principles of Christ lead to great achievements.

As David walked into the battle in the Valley of Eli to face Goliath, if he was so confident and he had so much faith in his slingshot and so much faith in his slingshot ability, why in the world did he take a staff? I once preached a message that I titled, "The Top of the Staff." This is where we see the value of a staff. It was a biblical custom that every time something of importance happened in a man's life, every time something of significance took place, he would take a knife and make a notch, a mark, a symbol on his staff, starting at the bottom and working up. There are several tribes in Africa that still do this. They couldn't have diaries. They didn't have books. They wrote on scrolls. To keep a diary or a journal couldn't be done. You'd have to walk around with this boatload of papyrus under your arm. You couldn't do it. So, to make it simpler, they took the knife and marked notches, cuts, symbols on the staff. Every notch was symbolic, a memory of some important point in his life.

Moses didn't want to lead the children out of Egypt. God was finally tired of dealing with him and He asked him, "What do you have in your hand?" He said, "I have my staff." What did God tell him to do? Throw it down. See, when you lay down your life, then you can pick it back up. You may think it's going to turn into a snake to bite you, but the snake didn't bite him, did it?

No. Just like Moses who was a murderer, you may think your past will hinder you. You can't pick up what you don't lay down. You lay it down first, when you pick it up, it will not harm you and you can use it for the glory of God. You can't live a resurrected life until you have learned to live the crucified life. Until you lay down your life, you cannot pick it up.

We all have our notches, our battle scars, our memory sticks that remind us of the strength God has given us in the day of battle. The words of Psalm 23:4, written by David, have great significance. *Yea, though I walk through the valley of the shadow of death, I will fear no evil: for thou art with me; thy rod and thy staff they comfort me.*

Did you ever wonder how a stick could comfort somebody? Here's the real truth behind this verse. When you're walking through hell, when you're being beat up from every corner, isn't it nice to be able to look at the staff and say, "Oh, I remember God. God helped me there. He helped me survive that tragedy. He saved me from those who spoke evil of me. He delivered me out of that great dark place." We can look at our proverbial staff and remember and be comforted. What kind of a staff is that? It's the staff of situations overcome. When David wrote the twenty-third psalm, he'd been to hell and back several times, and God had brought him through every time. His staff reminded him of those victories.

Sword of Past Successes

On the wall of that Davidic gallery of remembrance was a sword. The guards probably looked at that sword and said that it was the biggest sword they had ever seen and wondered where it came from. Like all the weapons on the wall, it was special and had a story. Take a look at that sword. Wow, I've never seen a sword like that. The story of that sword is found in 1 Samuel 21. David was running from Saul—his life in grave danger. He arrived at the city of Nob. Once he entered the city, he found Ahimelech the priest.

The priest was a little nervous about this meeting and wondered what David wanted with him. David told him to relax and that he was only there on business. While talking, David asked him if he had some bread hidden under his garments. The priest told him he did and gave David the bread to eat. After eating the bread, David noticed that the priest was hiding something else under his ephod and asked him if it was a sword. You never know what those old boys had hidden under their ephod.

He reached under that old ephod and pulled out something that the Bible says was wrapped in a cloth. And then, David said, "Man, what do you have there?" He unwrapped that thing and, lo and behold, it was a sword. That old preacher was carrying a sword. Now he's my kind of guy. But see, it wasn't just any sword. David looked at it and he said, "I recognize that." And the priest said, "You ought to. It's Goliath's sword. It's the sword that you used many years ago to cut off the head of your enemy." The weapon David used as a little boy is the same weapon he could now use as a grown man, because it still had the same power.

Just because you're older doesn't mean you have to trade in your old weapons for a new set of weapons. This sword was the sword of past success. What had worked in the past would still be useful today.

The great thing about winning a battle is that you can retell that story over and over and it still seems new. We all know how Alcoholics Anonymous meetings operate and they are all usually the same. Some person will get up and say, "My name is Joe. I'm an alcoholic. I've been sober for one year." What are they doing? They're recognizing their past condition and establishing their present success. It is good to take up the sword of the Lord and declare our past victories. It's the sword of past successes.

David looked at that sword and it reminded him of the goodness of the Lord. While Saul was trying to take his life, while there were agents of Saul all around him, he was reminded in that moment of his past success, and it gave him courage for this present moment. The weapons of our warfare are not carnal; they are mighty and pull down strongholds.

I shouldn't even be around today. I should be dead, and yet, I have survived to fight another day. When I think of His goodness and what He's done for me, it makes me want to shout and dance.

Shield of Encouragement

Hanging on the wall in the hall of honor was another weapon, a shield. As the priest took the shield off the wall, I am sure he looked at it and wondered where it came from. The shield was well worn, and had doubtless, been used in many a battle. There were not only sword marks and dents from David's battles, but there were stains of tears. The shield was unlike the other weapons. It was not an offensive weapon, but a defensive weapon, a weapon of protection. We are not sure where David's shield came from. In 2 Samuel 8:7 it says that David took the shields from the servants of Hadadezer, who he had killed in battle. When David had gone to Ziklag to make it his home base, 1 Chronicles 12:8 says that the men of Gad joined him at Ziklag. Concerning these soldiers, it is stated that they were fierce warriors and came to David with their swords and shields.

In 1 Samuel 30, we read of a painful story in the life of David. While David and his men were away, the Amalekites came in, burned down the city and kidnapped many of the sons, daughters and wives, leaving the city in mourning. When David and his men arrived and saw the condition of the city, they dropped their swords and shields and fell to the ground. They began to cry over their loss, until they couldn't cry anymore.

All of a sudden, everybody turned on David, blaming him for the actions of the Amalekites. The cry for action escalated to the point where they were ready to stone him. He had promised them that this would be a safe zone and now look what had happened.

David retreated from the crowd so he could be alone. In verse 6 we read, *And David was greatly distressed; for the people spake of stoning him, because the soul of all the people was grieved, every man for his sons and for his daughters: but David encouraged himself in the LORD his God.* David had to get his focus back, had to lift his eyes off the circumstances and find some encouragement. He encouraged himself in the Lord.

People are a fickle bunch. When you have success they will cheer, but when you fail they will crucify you. If you are a leader, you need to understand that there will come a point when you will be criticized. It is the nature of the beast. If you stand for something, there will be those that stand against you. *"First, recognize that criticism comes with leadership. You're a leader. Your leadership will be scrutinized, idolized, and criticized. Scrutinized, because your work is done in public; idolized, because your work is done on a pedestal; criticized, because your work is done with people, whom you can't please all the time."*[4]

David just walked away quietly. He put down the shield. He put down the sword, and he didn't know what to do. Will he give in to these accusations and give up, or will he find a way to move forward? The sorrow and accusations experienced at Ziklag drove David to the Lord, rather than the place of shame. In that heavenly abode, he was able to encourage himself in the Lord.

It's nice to have somebody there to encourage you. I've always wished I had more of that. It's always nice to have somebody applauding you. It's always nice when people say, "You're doing a good job." I have made every effort to applaud the efforts of others and encourage them when they succeeded or failed. Maybe it's because, in secret, I wish somebody would have done it for me when I was young, but nobody did. It's nice to have somebody stand with you. It's nice to have somebody encourage you. But if you don't have it, what do you do? You encourage yourself in the Lord. He is a faithful friend and will always be there for you.

I remember when I preached at the Hoosier Dome. I don't know how many people were there, probably thirty or forty-thousand people. I got a standing ovation for ten or fifteen minutes. I signed books till two o'clock in the morning. It was great. When I went out the side exit door to go back to the hotel, my car was the last car in the parking lot. I drove back to the hotel alone. The life of a leader is a lonely life, and if they do not learn to encourage themselves in the Lord, they are in trouble.

Take up the shield of self-encouragement. Let that shield protect you from the hurtful words and actions of others. Let it shield you from the discouragement. Let it shield you from the disillusionment of the ministry. Let it shield you from the heartbreak caused by people who don't understand all that you have been through. Let it catch your tears. You will not always bask in the sunlight of people's praise. There will be days when you are forced to live under the dark clouds of people's reproach. In those days, take up that protective shield of encouragement and shake off the disparagement of others.

Sheath of Adullam

There's one more thing on the wall I want to take a look at. The tour's almost finished. What's that hanging on the wall? It doesn't look like it belongs there. It shouldn't be there. It's an old empty sheath, a scabbard that carries the sword. It's empty. I wonder what story is behind that sheath. Let's bring it off the wall and take a look at it. I think it comes from the story over in 2 Samuel 23. As a matter of fact, I'm confident it is. In 2 Samuel 23:1 it says, *Now these be the last words of David.*

His life was coming to a close now and he was sitting in a cave, Adullam's cave. He was thinking about the great wars he has fought and the men who battled with him. Among those great warriors were a group of thirty men that I call David's mighty warriors. What an eclectic group of people. One killed three hundred at a time. The other one killed seven hundred. This unique group was a crazy bunch of die-hard warriors who had committed their lives to him. These mighty men were the soldiers who made up David's elite guard. They were his special forces trained in all the weapons of warfare and known for their great exploits.

Three of these men joined David at the cave of Adullam. The Philistines were encamped in Bethlehem, near the cave where David was entrenched. While in the cave, David spoke these words, almost in a whisper, in verse 15. *And David longed, and said, Oh that one would give me drink of the water of the well of Bethlehem, which is by the gate!* Four veteran soldiers, including David, were sitting in a cave, and, in the midst of their conversations, David uttered a wish. I don't think it was directly spoken to the other three. In a moment of silence, thinking of the cool waters in the well of Bethlehem, he sighed and murmured his coveted desire for a cup of that water.

One of these men said, "Hey, psst. Did you hear that?" David wasn't talking to them but one of them heard his yearning. These old warriors were tuned in to David's heart. The old warrior told the others, "Let's go get the old man a cup of water." Not an easy task. They had to break through the Philistine army, get to the well, drop down the bucket, draw up the water, dip the cup in the water, and fight their way back to David. They make it back. Arriving at the cave, so joyous about their success, they give the cup of water to David.

Now, here is the strange part of the story, only strange if you do not understand honor and loyalty. He took the cup of water and, in front of his men, poured it on the ground. Now, if I was one of those three guys I would think, *What did he just do? After all we went through and he just pours it out.*

Why did he throw that water out? Because, when you come to the end of your life, you look at life differently. It wasn't about the water. If he were to drink the water and say, "Thank you," that would have been the end of the story. It was a nice deed. It was an acceptable response. But he poured it out. Why? Here was David's response to that legitimate question in verse 17. *And he said, Be it far from me, O LORD, that I should do this: is not this the blood of the men that went in jeopardy of their lives? therefore he would not drink it. These things did these three mighty men.* In a sense, he was saying that he was not worthy to drink of that cup that was given with such great love and sacrifice. The water did not mean as much as the gratitude and honor he had for the loyalty and love of these war-worn soldiers.

When you're sitting in a cave, at the end of your life, and you're surrounded by friends, you don't need weapons anymore. David now had a company of men that would fight on his behalf. They had fought alongside of David. They have proved their value, their valor and their vows of commitment. He could now hang up all his weapons of war, because he now had people that would fight for him.

I have entered into the final phase of my life and you know what I am thankful for? I am thankful that I have a company of men and women who have stood with me and fought on my behalf. Through the tears, the fears, and the struggles, they have been here as faithful friends. I no longer have to worry about the ongoing success of this ministry. Many have been raised up who can now fight the battle on their own and on my behalf. They have picked up the mantle, they have the anointing, and they have been captured by my vision. I am certain that they will complete this work.

I have created a room for them, a place where I have hung my weapons, so that when they are needed, they can be taken down and used to fight their own battles. Not anybody could just pick those up and know what to do with them.

Someone has gone before you and fought their battles. They have paved a way for you and left a legacy of victories and an armory of weapons for the next generation. These men and women knew that a day would come when you would need those weapons to fight your own battles. They put them up, so that you could take them down in your time of need. These weapons are not weapons of this world. They are spiritual weapons, used by those in the past, and now presented to you. They will never be lost. They will be available for future times.

One day there will come a time in the history of the nation and the history of the Church that a new band of leaders will need to go into that room and take down those proven weapons.

> *Oh! I have seen the day*
> *When with a single word,*
> *God helping me to say*
> *"My trust is in the Lord,"*
> *My soul has quelled a thousand foes,*
> *Fearless of all that could oppose.*[5]

Chapter 10

Saving a Generation: If Jehosheba Doesn't Get Him, Athaliah Will

The ultimate test of man's conscience may be his
willingness to sacrifice something today for future
generations whose words of thanks will not be heard.[1]

I n the last chapter we looked at the story of Jehosheba and Athaliah and the plan to bring back the king. In this chapter I will zero in on a particular aspect of the story, saving the next generation. Athaliah sought to kill off the next generation, while Jehosheba worked to save it.

It has been my passion and devotion to leave a mark on the next generation. Everything I do ultimately reflects my commitment to this cause. I don't seek to build a monument to myself. I seek to build a future for those who will come after me. The sacrifices I have made, the battles I have fought, and the successes I have experienced have only one goal: to save the next generation.

We need to reevaluate the essence of the urgency of what we do. The pressure of the urgency of the moment is always with me. I never want it to be commonplace. Before "now" slips away, I must be certain that all I do is contributing to the cause of Christ in the future.

Let us review the story and then we will look at five important points that will help us save a nation.

Athaliah had lost her way and was consumed with a desire to own the throne. Her selfishness and addiction to power caused her to become blind to the next generation. In the vacuum created by Ahaziah's death, she sought to kill the next generation and seize the throne.

Usually a grandmother would be the first one to take care of the children. The lust for power caused her to lose her motherly instincts. This didn't happen by accident. Jezebel, another wicked queen, was the mother of Athaliah. I have often said to those who are considering marriage, if you want to know what your future wife will be like, look at her mother.

She had killed all the grandkids, except one, and that one was Jehoash. If it were not for Jehosheba and her husband/priest Jehoida, he would have been slaughtered. Both of them recognized the urgency of the situation. At this point, they knew that the royal blood line was about to be destroyed forever. They knew something had to be done. Before Athaliah could get her hands on Jehoash, Jeshosheba stole him away and hid him in the temple. For seven years he was under her protection. At the end of the seven years, Jehoida initiated the plan that we saw played out in chapter nine.

Five key players are involved in this narrative: the murdered king, his greedy mother, the priest, the priest's wife, and the young boy that was saved. They did not know if their plan would work, but they knew they had to do something to save the next generation. The kingdom was now in their hands. The entire future of a nation could be won or lost on the decision of one person who saw and acted. The great ones always see the need and create a plan for that need.

Here was a nation hinging on what they did at this moment in their lives. If Jehosheba didn't get him, Athaliah would. If we don't protect and preserve this generation, others will destroy them. Ronald Raegan cautioned our generation with these haunting words. "*Freedom is never more than one generation away from extinction. We didn't pass it to our children in the bloodstream. It must be fought for, protected, and handed on for them to do the same.*"[2]

There's an issue of urgency in the world and in our nation today. I'm not talking about communist and socialist countries, and I'm not talking about Muslim nations. I am talking OUR nation. Our children have been taken from our homes, sent to school, where existential, atheistic professors are indoctrinating them with the philosophies of this world. They are killing their spirit and stealing their faith.

> The choices and decisions we make in this generation will impact future generations.

I may have grown up in a different generation than you. Our nation has lost its moral compass, as it drifts away into the seas of secularism. I remember watching a television news program discussing the state of our nation and these words of one of the participants left me shaking my head in agreement. "*Christians at this time in world history do not care enough to step up and be counted.*" I agree with this assessment. We are not fighting for the next generation, and if we are not careful, we will lose them.

I feel that urgency every day that I wake up. I am compelled by the love for my generation and the next. I am not looking for a successor. I am looking for some willing hands that will help me pass the torch to the next generation. The choices and decisions we make in this generation will impact future generations.

Moment of Opportunity

There was a generation at risk. The kingdom was at stake. There was an urgency. And, thank God, somebody saw it. Thank God, somebody recognized it and had enough drive, quickness, and enough foresight, insight, and vision to say, "If I don't do something, our future is lost. It's over."

In the every hour of urgency, there will be a moment of opportunity. When we're considering the urgency, and we look at how fragile the kingdom of God is, we see how easily a nation can be destroyed. We must have eyes to see the opportunities that are ours in order to save a generation. Our great danger at this time is that we might miss our moment of opportunity.

I have spoken with my staff many times about the Italian merchant traveler from Venice, Marco Polo (1254-1324), and his experiences in China. It was a few months before Marco was born that his father Niccolo and his uncle Maffeo left Venice on a trading trip to Asia. In the diary of Marco Polo, *The Travels of Marco Polo*, we are given details of the first trip his father and uncle made to China, as well as the future trips that young Marco made with them.

The Polo brothers traveled for a year before they arrived at the court of Kublai Kahn (1215-1294). When the two brothers got to the Great Khan, he received them into his presence with honor and hospitality.

Khan was curious to hear about the land from which they came. He asked them questions about their emperor, their government and laws, and their battles. Then he asked them about their Pope and the Christian religion. In great detail, the brothers told Kahn about the history of Christianity and the Catholic Church. Kahn was enthralled with the stories of Christ and the great leaders of the Church.

A momentous opportunity was being unveiled to the Polo brothers. At the end of their conversation we read, in the writings of Marco Polo, about an unusual request from the Khan, the prince of China. *"He begged that the Pope would send as many as a hundred persons of our Christian faith; intelligent men, acquainted with the seven arts, well qualified to enter into controversy, and able clearly to prove by force of argument to idolaters and other kinds of folk, that the law of Christ was best, and that all other religions were false and naught; and that if they would prove this, he and all under him would become Christians."*[3]

The brothers returned to Italy with Kahn's request. They arrived to see the Holy See in great chaos. Pope Clement IV (1190-1268) had died. It took three years for Pope Gregory X (1210-1276) to take the Papal throne. This vacancy delayed the Polo brothers in fulfilling the Kahn's request. Marco's father did not feel the urgency of the moment. He remained in Italy until there was someone in power to answer the Kahn's request. Finally, they were ready to leave and would take young Marco with them. The new Pope only sent two friars with them, and they brought a bottle of holy water. Along the way, the two friars gave up and returned home. *"The Pope chose two friars—in place of the one hundred men the Khan asked for—to accompany the Polos on their journey and sent many fine gifts as well. The two friars, the book says, were the wisest in all that province. But neither was ready for the risk of travels beyond Christendom. Frightened for this life, the friars quickly arranged a return to Acre.*"[4]

Here is the tragic picture. First, it took five years to get back to the Kahn's court, and they arrived with not one spiritual person that the Kahn had requested. They come with holy water, but no missionaries to teach them the ways of Christ. Secondly, they are delayed by squabbles among the Cardinals in choosing the next pope. The church at Rome was also distracted by the ongoing Crusades in Israel. Church squabbles and church wars contributed to missing a great opportunity in China. Not one single soul saw the urgency of the moment.

> There will come a time when you have a chance to make a difference in the life of someone that will have great impact on others.

Flash forward to the present. Today, one out of every four people in this world is Chinese. We had a moment of opportunity in world history to bring the Gospel to a country that would end up becoming the largest people group in the world. Because mistakes were made, opportunities were ignored, and the chance to change the historical course of a nation and the world was lost.

Jehoiada and Jehosheba recognized the urgency of their moment and responded with courage and commitment. Will you recognize your moment of urgency? How will you respond? Believe me; you will have a moment that will demand your attention. You can call it a moment of destiny. You can call it a crossroads. You can call it whatever you want, but will you see it? Maybe you won't see the magnitude of the moment, but there will come a time when you have a chance to make a difference in the life of someone that will have great impact on others. If you are so consumed with other things and you're not looking for it, you will miss it just as Marco Polo and his father did, and as so many other people in the church world have for centuries. You will be held accountable for that moment. You will be held responsible for that moment. It is my prayer that you will not miss YOUR moment.

Throughout history there have been moments of opportunity, private moments that most people will never know. In those moments there is an urgency to act. A world waits on that moment. Such was the story in the life of Dwight L. Moody (1837-1899), the great evangelist.

It was 1855. A young man in Northfield, Massachusetts was attending the Sunday School class of Mr. Edward Kimble. Kimble was attracted to the young man and burdened to tell him about Christ. *"Mr. Kimble went to the shoe store where the 18-year-old D.L. Moody was a clerk and led him to saving faith in Jesus Christ."*[5]

Did Kimble, as he walked toward the shoe store that day, know what he was going to say? Was there an urgency in his witness and did he understand the importance of what he was doing? *Be careful, Mr. Kimble, because the United States is hinging on what you do when you walk into that shoe store.* We never know how significant a seemingly insignificant moment can become. Mr. Kimble's compassion and burden for young Moody led him into that store and when he walked out, Moody had entered the Kingdom! Kimble's response to the moment became the catalyst of a worldwide revival through the ministry of Dwight L. Moody. It is said that Moody took a continent in each hand and shook them for Christ.

The story doesn't quite end here. The British preacher and theologian, F.B. Meyer (1847-1929), was greatly impacted and inspired by the preaching of Moody. Nineteenth-century Presbyterian evangelist Wilbur Chapman (1859-1918) found Christ in Meyer's meetings in the USA. While Chapman was preaching in the famous Pacific

Garden Mission in Chicago, a drunken baseball player stumbled into his meetings. At the end of that meeting, Billy Sunday gave his life to the Lord. In 1924 some businessmen invited Sunday to have an evangelistic crusade in the city of Charlotte. From that meeting a group of men formed a prayer meeting that prayed for revival in their city. In 1934 that group invited Mordecai Hamm (1877-1961) to hold revival services there. During those services a tall, skinny young man gave his life to the Lord. That man was Billy Graham (1918-). Now, you know the rest of the story.[6]

Years of Preparation

A moment of opportunity was followed by years of preparation. Jehosheba took the young boy and hid him away for six years in the temple. For six years, the kid was introduced to life in the temple. He heard the Scriptures, experienced the worship, saw the sacrifices, and was exposed to the commitment of the priests to maintain the worship of Jehovah. The little boy was silently being taught, quietly being trained, secretly being developed, because one day his time would come to take the throne. Timing was everything. Training had to precede the throne.

> Champions are not born in a day.

Champions are not born in a day. It takes years of training and preparation. "Champions do not become champions when they win the event, but in the hours, weeks, months and years they spend preparing for it. The victorious performance itself is merely the demonstration of their championship character."[7] In a critical and momentous moment a life is selected and protected for their future destiny. Before that life can embrace their calling, there must be a preparation, training for the approaching season. Sixteenth President of the United States Abraham Lincoln (1809-1865) said that he prepared himself for the day that would come. Ben Franklin (1706-1790) said that if you fail to prepare, you are preparing to fail. Success awaits the ones who have prepared themselves wisely.

Susanna Wesley (1669-1742) is one of my favorite women of the Word. I'd like to have been the person who told her: "Be careful for your moment is here. The little boy you're rocking in your arms in that rocking chair will one day rock a nation. Be careful what you say to him. Be careful how you train him, because you don't know it today, but there is a nation that's sitting on your lap." Susanna Wesley didn't have to be told, though. She recognized her moment.

Susanna diligently educated all of her children and especially John (1703-1791). She instilled in all of her children a love for God and commitment to His purposes. At the age of six, John Wesley was rescued from the burning rectory where his father was pastor. John would call that moment "a brand plucked from the burning." Susanna made a habit of spending one evening a week with each child separately. The evening she spent with John was precious and focused, seeing in his miraculous escape from the fire a sign of destiny on his life.

At John Wesley's request, Susanna wrote him a letter that contained her philosophy and actions on the education of her family. In that letter she mentioned some of the key practices she initiated in the training of her kids. "The children of this family were taught, as soon as they could speak, the Lord's Prayer, which they were made to say at rising and bedtime constantly. They were made to distinguish the Sabbath from other days."[8]

Susanna Wesley laid the foundation in the life of her son, who would become one of the greatest spiritual reformers in the history of Great Britain, Ireland, and North America.

A Week to Assemble

We are looking at some critical and necessary points to saving a generation. The next one I call "a week to assemble." That is the time designated to implement the plan. Jehoiada knew that the changing of the guard happened on the Sabbath. The replacements for the palace guards came in at the changing of the guard. They had to stay there throughout the day until the evening. Then those who were replacing them took over the guard. So Jehoiada knew the largest collection—the largest group of army personnel—would be gathered in one place on the Sabbath during that shift change.

During the week leading up to the Sabbath, he made the final plans, rehearsing the strategies with all that would be involved. There was a week to put the plan together, a final week to prepare. The most important part of the plan was making sure the selected guard knew their part in guarding the young king. No one would be allowed to break through to him. These mighty men would give up their lives, if needed, to protect the coming king. There was a moment of opportunity. There were years of preparation. There was a week to put the final plan in place.

Carpe diem! Seize the day. All the time of preparation led us to the day when the plan, the goal must be activated. American playwright and essayist Arthur Miller (1915-2005) once said that the word *now* is like a bomb through the window, and it ticks. When the *now* of opportunity arrives, there is no time for delay. The future has arrived and *now* is the time to act. To delay is dangerous.

Be careful, Johann Trebonius. You're just a school teacher. You don't think that what you do counts for much. But you have no idea that sitting in your classroom today is a little boy named Martin Luther.

Trebonius was a gifted scholar and teacher at St. George's school in Eisenach, Germany. When Luther was 14, his father sent him to St. George, and he came under the influence of Trebonius. "The principal teacher was Johann Trebonius, a man of good parts but somewhat eccentric. He always removed his cap upon entering the school room because he knew not what great man might be before him in the persons of one those boys."[9] Because of the influence of one man, the fires of reformation would be lit by a young boy that sat in his class.

Hour of Confrontation

Next came the hour of confrontation. There will be a moment of opportunity. There will be years of preparation. There will be a time to assemble, but there will come the hour of confrontation. That hour was now. They brought the child out. The crowd was ecstatic. It was a new king. He was a little boy, only seven years old. The young king stood patiently as they put the crown on his head and a shout of joy erupted. From her rooms in the palace, Athaliah heard the noise. She ran over to the window to see what was going on. The guards had already been put in place. The preparation had been made. Jehoiada was there. Jehosheba was there. The little boy

> Every victory in life demands a deliberate action, a confrontation.

had the crown on his head, and Athaliah saw what was happening. And she yelled, "Treason! Treason! Treason!"

It was the moment of truth—the hour of confrontation. At the instructions of the priest, the guards seized Athaliah, took her outside the city and killed her.

There will come a time when all of your work, all of your labor, all of the preparation, time and effort will come to that point of consummation. You have worked hard to get to that point. Don't miss it.

When the moment arrives in your life, you have two choices. You either confront your enemy or you flee from your enemy. Fight or flight, those are the choices. Your whole life conspires to bring you to the point of this decision. What will you do in the moment of opportunity that you have been prepared for? Every victory in life demands a deliberate action, a confrontation. The decision you make in that moment could make history.

Be careful, lay preacher in Colchester, England. You're just a lay preacher. You're not licensed. You're not ordained, but you have a message that you must deliver to that little primitive Methodist church. There will be a fifteen-year-old young man in that meeting. This is the hour of confrontation for that young man, and you will be the messenger.

The little village was in the middle of a major snow storm. The weather was so bad the pastor didn't even show up. They were going to dismiss the service, but fifteen people were actually there, along with the lay preacher, and the young man. No one in the church knew that history would be made that day. The name of that young boy was Charles Haddon Spurgeon (1834-1892). Spurgeon had visited many churches in the city, looking for someone to tell him how to be saved. He found no solace for his soul in those churches. Finally, the hour of confrontation came for a layman and Spurgeon. Here is how Spurgeon described that day, in his own words.

"I sometimes think I might have been in darkness and despair until now, had it not been for the goodness of God in sending a snowstorm one Sunday morning, while I was going to a certain place of worship. I turned down a side street, and came to a little Primitive Methodist Church. In that chapel there may have been a dozen or fifteen people.

"The minister did not come that morning; he was snowed up, I suppose. At last a very thin-looking man, a shoemaker, or tailor, or something of that sort, went up into the pulpit to preach. Now it is well that preachers be instructed, but this man was really stupid. He was obliged to stick to his text, for the simple reason that he had little else to say. The text was—LOOK UNTO ME, AND BE YE SAVED, ALL THE ENDS OF THE EARTH (Isaiah 45:22).

"He did not even pronounce the words rightly, but that did not matter. There was, I thought, a glimmer of hope for me in that text."

On that momentous day, Spurgeon went on to say that the clouds had rolled away and the darkness was gone, and he could now see the sun. He could have risen at that moment and sang enthusiastically of the blood of Jesus.

Why do you think I still preach at small churches? Nobody in my position does that. Not anymore. They all want to go to the big ones. I learned something a long time ago. When I first came to New York, all those years ago, the only churches that would invite me were those little churches. Most preachers start out that way, but when they rise to the place of fame, they never go back. Not me! I still have a passion for those places, for you see, you never know what life you might reach. Never despise the places you might be called to speak. That layman did not know that the young man that found Christ on that Sunday morning would go on to speak to over 10 million people. Nor do you know what influence you might have in your hour of confrontation.

Day of Restoration

The throne had been saved and restored through the commitment and actions of a priest and his wife. What originally had been taken was restored. The wicked queen's plot to destroy a generation had been foiled. This couple and the brave warriors that stood with them brought back the king and restored the throne. This isn't just an interesting Bible narrative. Behind the story, there is a truth here. There's a truth here of the urgency of a nation, an urgency of a generation at risk. If we don't stand up for them, who will? A life saved could be a life that changes a world.

You had better be careful, teachers. Those you are teaching understand exactly what you're saying. Don't think they don't. Don't think that they are too young to be influenced by your words and actions.

He was four years old, and on that particular Sunday a little boy went to the altar and knelt to pray in a Scottish church. His heart was moved by the words he heard that day. He was just a little boy. Did he understand what he was doing? Not only was he ignored, he was despised for his action. That little boy was Robbie Moffat. Here is a short account of that day.

"It seemed a small thing to some godly men in a southern Scotland church when a boy about four years old, from a home of poor but pious parents, knelt at an altar to pray. His decision was despised by the elders as one who was too young to understand. Thank God, one unnamed, unknown-to-us brother bothered to kneel in prayer with Robbie.

"Moffat may well have been converted to Christ then—if not, it was the commencement of a chain of events that led to his conversion and to the opening of doors of evangelism to the uncharted depths of the dark continent of Africa."[10]

Robert Moffat (1795-1883) would grow up and make history in Africa. He arrived in Cape Town, South Africa in 1817 and labored in South Africa for 51 years. He and his wife experienced much

> Recognize the urgency of the moment. Create your own plan of action.

hardship and heartache in those primitive lands. Three of their children died while in Africa, but Mary, their oldest daughter, married the renowned David Livingstone (1813-1873), the famed Scottish Congregational pioneer, medical missionary, and explorer in Africa. Moffat's labor in Africa would become the stepping stone for many others to spread the Gospel throughout Africa.

So, you never know how your simple acts and words might touch a life and restore a nation. You might not preach to thousands, but you can influence one child who will reach thousands. Do not despise the smallness of what you do. You just might be the key to saving a generation. Recognize the urgency of the moment. Create your own plan of action. If you can save just one life, it will be worth it. Who knows? Maybe that life will be the next Spurgeon, or Moody or Moffat. Be careful. There may be a Bill Wilson at that altar. Nobody wanted to pray with me either.

There's a generation dying. Twenty-four thousand die from starvation every day. How does that work? In a world where there's plenty of food, 24,000 kids are dying. We cannot sit idly by while a whole generation is lost. We must act. We must sacrifice. If we miss a step, the whole nation fails. People are more worried about the environment than they are worried about children. Governments spend billions of dollars on frivolous things to preserve our lives at a time when our chief concern should be influencing and saving the next generation.

Our future is in the hands of the next generation. Let us save them, prepare them, encourage them and inspire them to become all they can be in their momentous times of opportunity. We cannot wait until tomorrow. Now is the time to save the next generation!

Chapter 11

Learning to Keep Rank: If You Don't Know How to Fight, Go Home

"Commitment doesn't have conditions. A compassionate samurai follows through whether it feels good or not; average people do what they feel like doing. The historical samurai kept their commitments even if it cost them their lives." [1]

D r. Martin Luther King had a dream, but that dream was more than a fascination. He converted that dream into action. The combination of dream and deed caused him to be one of the great leaders in the history of this country. Because of his compassionate commitment to the dream, backed up by incredible achievement, an army of men and women followed him in the elevation and evolution of the dream.

David had a dream to be king of Israel and to establish Israel as the exclusive worshipers of Yahweh. His dream drove him to the battlefield and made him notorious for his exploits. In the process of fulfilling his dream, a company of mighty men became his followers. Their level of commitment and dedication to David made them famous, as well.

> Real leadership is about influence and persuasion, not position and prestige.

This is really the essence of leadership. Leadership, as we define it in today's culture, especially the American culture, is not real leadership at all. We tend to identify leadership with position. Just because you have a position over people does not mean you are a leader.

Contrary to public opinion, real leadership is not appointed, elected or enthroned. Real leadership is when someone is doing something of their own volition, and chooses to follow that person because of who they are, what they do, what they know, and because of where they're going. One of the problems of democracy is that there are too many times when ill-informed people elect ill-equipped people.

Real leadership is about influence and persuasion, not position and prestige. Billy Graham illustrates my point. Graham was not appointed or elected to be an evangelist. His calling was from a higher source. If you've ever listened to any of his messages, he's not what many of us would consider a deep theological orator. The central theme of his message was personal commitment to Christ. It was a simple message, but delivered with great anointing. "Billy (William Franklin) Graham was the most preeminent Protestant leader in the second half of the twentieth century ... Graham's influence was enormous—from the White House (where he consulted with a number presidents) to other nations. Graham asserted, undoubtedly correctly, that he preached to more people than anyone else in history—215 million people in more than 185 countries."[2]

I doubt that there will ever be anyone like him again. His simple message of conversion to Christ influenced people in Hollywood and people in Washington D.C., people in Nashville and people in Boston, prostitutes and drug addicts, rich people and poor people. He powerfully demonstrated the true essence of leadership.

After David defeated Goliath, he began to attract many of the warriors that once fought in Saul's army. In fact, from all the tribes of Israel, they came to David and surrendered their lives to him. In 1 Chronicles 12 we are introduced to a specific group that became known as David's mighty men. *Now these are they that came to David to Ziklag, while he yet kept himself close because of Saul the son of Kish: and they were among the mighty men, helpers of the war.*

In 1 Chronicles 12 we see a list of those mighty men and their characteristics. This group of unique individuals that were following him was not your ordinary group of folk. They arrived in David's camp with special abilities and special weapons. They would become the core of David's army that would defeat the Philistines and eventually get David to his throne. In this chapter, I want to share with you some key points about these men and how they relate to leadership in our times.

They Understood the Times

And of the children of Issachar, which were men that had understanding of the times, to know what Israel ought to do; the heads of them were two hundred; and all their brethren were at their commandment.

—1 Chronicles 12:32

They understood the significance of the time in which they were living. They understood that a major paradigm shift was happening, a shift that would eventually bring David to the throne. They were well versed in political and national affairs and with prophetic eyes they could see a future where David would replace Saul. These men were leaders and were willing to surrender their leadership to David because they saw in him the next great king, a king after God's own heart.

> Great leaders will attract other leaders, those with discernment and awareness of the cultural issues of our time.

Great leaders will attract other leaders, those with discernment and awareness of the cultural issues of our time. They are able to see through the smog of deception and dishonesty that permeates the times in which we live.

David tried to surround himself with men and women who understood what was going on. These men understood the culture and knew what needed to be done. That's why every week I read magazines, books and newspapers. I want to keep up to date on the times that we are living in. I seek to understand the myths, the trends, the lies and the dangers in our culture, and I want to be surrounded by people who also have the same kind of understanding and discernment. I have tried to create a company of folk that understand the movements of our age and who will fight with me to cure the cancers in our culture.

Unfortunately, Christians are some of the most ignorant people in the world. They have no concept of the world and what's going on around them. They have little discernment because their eyes are on their own issues, rather than the problems that plague our world. You need to know what's going on, so you can understand the times in which we live. If you don't understand it, you are not going to know how people think and why they think that way. We must have a new brand of people who have discernment and wisdom and are able to confront the shifting shadows of corruption, deception and moral ambiguity.

Tolkien's second book of the *Lord of the Rings* was entitled *The Two Towers*. In that second book there is an interesting conversation between Eomer and his friends. Their conversation centers around a question and a comment about good and evil. "*Eomer gives voice to a surprisingly modern-sounding uncertainty complaining: 'It is hard to be sure of anything among so many marvels... How shall a man judge what to do in such times?'*"[3]

After several rounds of discussion, Aragorn enters the conversation and through the pen of Tolkien answers the question. "*Good and evil have not changed since yesteryear. Nor are they one thing among elves and dwarves and another among men. It is a man's part to discern as much in The Golden Wood, as in his own home.*"[4]

In another part of the dialog, Aagorn is talking with the dwarfs and makes this powerful statement as his concluding resolve. "*Let me think! And now I make a right choice, and change the evil of this unhappy.*"[5] There is no moral relativism or hesitation on the difference between right and wrong in the writings of Tolkien. How shall a man judge *in these times?* Tolkien gives us the right answer and it works for us in these times. It is man's part to discern the times and to make a right choice. The sons of Issachar were of the ilk of a Tolkien story. Like Aragorn, they understood what needed to be done and did it.

They Were Experts at War

They were among the mighty men, helpers of the war...

—1 Chronicles 12:1

And of the Gadites there separated themselves unto David into the hold to the wilderness men of might, and men of war fit for the battle...

—1 Chronicles 12:8

Of Zebulun, such as went forth to battle, expert in war...

—1 Chronicles 12:33

These warriors that joined David at Ziklag were not fresh out of boot camp. They were expert warriors that had already fought many battles. They were no strangers to the art of ancient warfare. David did not attract people who were mediocre at war. He needed experts. There is a great difference between men who have just graduated from military academy and soldiers who have spent twenty years in war. Training is important, but it is no substitute for experience.

That's our goal here in New York. I need people who know how to fight. I need people who have made it their business to know how to do battle with the enemy. I want people who have some battle scars, who have fought many wars and have looked into the eye of the enemy and not retreated. Unseasoned men can be dangerous men, for they just might abandon you in the heat of battle. The world is desperate to see a new brand of warriors that are trained and equipped to take the battle to the very gates of hell.

In December 1944, 12,000 U.S. paratroopers laid siege and took over the town of Bostogne, Belgium. They were immediately surrounded by 15 divisions of German troops. Against all odds, those brave, experienced men were able to hold off the German troops until General Patton could arrive and save the day. This story was made into a very popular movie called "Band of Brothers." I am looking for a band of brothers—a company of trained warriors who are willing to join me in the battle to save our nation.

They Were Experts with All Weapons of War

They were armed with bows, and could use both the right hand and the left in hurling stones and shooting arrows out of a bow...
—1 Chronicles 12:2

...that could handle shield and buckler, whose faces were like the faces of lions, and were as swift as the roes upon the mountain.
—1 Chronicles 12:8

And these are the numbers of the bands that were ready armed to the war...
—1 Chronicles 12:23

Not only were these mighty men experts at war, they were expertly equipped with all kinds of weapons of war. As a band of brothers, they came to David ready and equipped to fight alongside the future king. These valiant men knew how to use the shield and the sword. They knew how to use a bow and arrow, and they were trained in the use of a spear. They were all equipped in the use of the weapons of their day.

> We need intercessors that will stand in the gap and fight spiritual forces in the high places.

In modern warfare, our soldiers are trained in the use of an M-16, tanks, fighter jets, sniper rifles, grenade launchers and many more. As I have said, we do not use carnal weapons, actual military weapons. We need men and women trained in spiritual weapons, the weapons of prayer and intercession, worship, deliverance, and the whole arsenal of the Holy Spirit.

In Ephesians 6:14-18, Paul outlines some of the key weapons of our warfare and they make sense: loins girt about with truth, the shield of faith, the helmet of salvation, the breastplate of righteousness, the boots of peace, the sword of the Spirit, and in all things, prayer.

In order to bring back the King in our lives and in our world, we need men and women equipped in the use of these weapons. We need people who are mature enough to recognize the lies and deception of the enemy. I want to find some folk that know how to take up the shield of faith to move some mountains. We need intercessors that will stand in the gap and fight spiritual forces in the high places. Finally, we need some valiant warriors who know how to wield the sword of the Spirit, which is the Word of God.

Besides these spiritual weapons, there is another armory we need to open. It is the armory of gifting. Our gifts take us to places where the weapons can be used and in a sense they are weapons also. Writers, educators, artists, musicians, videographers, entrepreneurs, experts in media, doctors—we need them all, experts in war and gifts, so that we can go forth into all the world and bring it back to Christ.

They Were Not of a Double Heart

... They were not of double heart.

—1 Chronicles 12:33

Besides being war-tested veterans, trained and tested on the battle field, they were men of a single heart. They were not of a heart and a heart, as the Hebrews would say. To say one was not of a double heart meant three things. They were loyal. They were honest. They were focused.

These men who joined David did not possess a double loyalty. They had cut their ties with Saul and with one heart they joined David. These men were soldiers who knew the importance of loyalty, allegiance, and faithfulness. They recognized and valued the necessity of being committed to a singular vision. They understood the cause to put David on the throne and had pledged their allegiance to the man and his mission.

They did not speak with forked-tongue. There was no deception in their words. *They speak vanity every one with his neighbour: with flattering lips and with a double heart do they speak* (Psalm 12:2). There was no deception in what these men were doing. They were not double agents sneaking into David's camp on behalf of Saul. Christian theologian Augustine (354-430) wrote that a person of deceitful lips is a person that does not have a "simple" heart. It is a heart and a heart. The person of a double heart will speak one thing to your face and another thing when you are not around. Those of a double heart are treacherous people and have ruined many people and ministries. Great leaders honor their word and understand the importance of honesty and loyalty.

A person of a double heart is an unfocused person. Another way to look at it is that a double-hearted person is a double-minded person. James 1:8 says that a double-minded man is unstable in all of his ways. Those ancient warriors came to David with a single heart, a single mind. There were no ulterior motives in their actions. Like a laser beam, they were focused on the cause before them. They had no other fascinations or distractions that would keep them from accomplishing the goal.

Being focused has two aspects: the ability to filter out distractions and the determination to focus attention on what is important. An undisciplined mind is not able to maintain this kind of focus.

> The key to becoming successful is learning what you are to do and then doing it with all your heart.

When you look at the leadership in the Bible, you'll see that they wanted to surround themselves with people who wanted to be the best at what they did. Focused people seek to excel in a few areas, rather than be good in a lot of areas. They don't dabble in a lot of interests; they focus on a few.

I am constantly trying to learn how to do things better. I am only content with excellence. I want people who have that same passion. I don't need people who are of a different heart and mind. The reason why I am doing what I'm doing today, at the level I'm doing it, is not because I'm smart, but because I am focused. I have picked one thing, and for over thirty years, I have hammered this thing out. I am not running around trying to save a world. I have spent my whole life trying to save one city. The key to becoming successful is learning what you are to do and then doing it with all your heart. Paulo Coelho put it this way, *"Whenever you want to achieve something, keep your eyes open, concentrate and make sure you know exactly what it is you want. No one can hit their target with their eyes closed."*[6]

They Could Keep Rank

Finally, in 1 Chronicles 12:33, it says that they could keep rank. Out of all the things we have said about these men, you might think that this is the most mundane. *Au contraire!* This might be the most important one. Unless you have been in the military, you probably will not understand this point. Keeping rank means to maintain a determined position in relationship to others, a series of individuals that are arranged side by side in order to a given purpose.

Marching in rank is not a modern-day war tactic, like it was in past wars. So, why do they still practice marching in boot camps? There is a specific answer to that question. Drill marching teaches soldiers to keep rank, to stay in unison, to obey orders, to learn teamwork, to understand unit cohesion and to have personal discipline. They do it hours upon hours until it is imbedded into their memory, and they can keep rank without thinking. How many times have we heard a soldier, recently returned from the war zone, talk about how he knows the soldier next to him has his back?

There's something powerful about a group of men and women all moving in the same direction, without distraction, and with purpose. We all love going to a parade and watching a marching band or a group of soldiers marching in unison. This is not what I am talking about. Keeping rank is not for parades; it is for the battlefield. What a soldier learns in boot camp could very well save his life in the war zone.

Do you remember watching some of those old war movies, where you saw one wave of soldiers after another coming at the enemy? When those water crafts hit the beach, the soldiers would hit the water, wading through it to get to the beach, with all kinds of enemy fire flying over their heads. No matter how many of their brothers were killed, they kept coming, wave after wave. That's why we won the war, because of the loyalty, focus and sacrifice of those young men.

Don't you think they were scared to death? Don't you think they wanted to stop? You know they did. It is human nature, but they were trained to do one thing; they had an objective. They were going somewhere, and they had an enemy to defeat.

Do you understand what I'm saying? You don't win a war by stopping because you got scared. You're trained, you know what to do and you know that everyone doing their part is the key to victory. They stood side by side with their brothers and fought till the enemy was defeated.

Our young people are not getting that kind of training in these days. We cram their heads with a lot of theological knowledge, but we don't teach them how to do battle, how to stay focused, how to keep rank and how to succeed. Part of the problem is that many of those professors have never learned those lessons. They have never experienced life outside the classroom. The only way you are going to get this kind of training is by being out on the field. You have to be knocked around a little, have some doors slammed in your face, experience being rejected and betrayed. Life has its own ways of teaching us and toughening us up.

In Vietnam 58,210 soldiers were killed in battle. Since the Vietnam War, more than 60,000 Vietnam War veterans have committed suicide. More have committed suicide than were killed in the battle. Why? They don't have a purpose any more. They don't have the camaraderie. They didn't know what to do with all their training. The same thing happens when people retire early. Many of them lose interest in life and die too soon.

What I am trying to say is that we were meant to live life with purpose and in synchronization with others. We were never meant to live a solitary life, devoid of meaning and interest. Before I end this chapter, I want to share five principles of how to keep rank in life.

They Did What They Were Commanded To Do

Keeping rank is about obedience, learning to do what you are commanded to do. This is not a very popular principle in the current culture we live in. Rebellion seems to be the order of the day, even when it is cloaked in spirituality. Christian author and speaker Elisabeth Elliot (1926-), that great warrior of God, wrote these words to those who would do battle for God. "Does it make sense to pray for guidance about the future if we are not obeying in the thing that lies before us today? How many momentous events in Scripture depended on one person's seemingly small act of obedience! Rest assured: Do what God tells you to do now, and, depend upon it, you will be shown what to do next."[7]

> There are always ways to do things better and improve things.

They kept on doing what they were commanded to do. They got in their position, they got in their spot, and they kept rank, and they stayed there until they were moved. I am convinced that advancement in life is dependent upon obedience in life. If we are faithful in the small things, we will be given more responsibility.

I've had the same position all my life, but through my faithfulness, I have enlarged the scope of that position. No position in life is too small for you. As you grow, your position will grow with you. There are always ways to do things better and improve things. Too many people want to move on to something higher and more exciting, not knowing that the very thing they seek is there for them.

Hebrews 5:8 says that Jesus *learned* obedience through the things He suffered. Obedience is not a natural thing. Submitting to God and others does not come easy. In the trials of life we learn the importance of obedience and the absurdity of selfishly pursuing our own pleasures.

Jesus commanded us to go into all the world and preach the Gospel of the kingdom. I have made that command my life's commitment. I have learned what it is to walk the way of obedience and so must you. Brokenness is not an experience; it is a way of life. Broken ones know the power and importance of obeying God and man.

They Didn't Turn Aside During the Battle

They didn't turn aside to fight other little skirmishes. They didn't get distracted by going after some stupid little skirmishes. When somebody came at them with a pea shooter, they didn't all run over there and kill the guy with the pea shooter. You are always going to have someone trying to heckle you and trying to get you side tracked. Don't get involved in little battles. Life is filled with all kind of battles. The experienced warrior knows how to pick his battles, discerning those that are more critical to the overall strategy for ultimate victory.

> We need to stand in rank and not allow ourselves to get involved in skirmishes.

The issue of abortion needs to be addressed and something needs to be done about the indiscriminate killing of the unborn, and some people have made this issue the primary battle of this time. Others have chosen to fight the liquor trade and make that a primary battle.

Listen, I hate it with a passion because it destroyed my family, killed my father, killed my mother, and probably would've killed me. I understand the battle against the legalization of homosexuality. I have made my stand quite clear, and my position is that it is ungodly and needs to be stopped.

But that's not our main battle, and I don't believe that is why we are here. We're here to bring people to Christ. We're here to get them delivered. And we're here to see them set free by the power of the Holy Ghost. The only hope for reversing the moral trend in our world is to change the hearts of men. This is where the battle is raging and it is the commitment we must make. That's why we're here. We need to stand in rank and not allow ourselves to get involved in skirmishes. We define the core of the battle and then throw ourselves into the heat of it.

They didn't turn aside to little skirmishes; they marched to the drum of the Master Drummer. The main job of a church is to march like an army, and keep moving, no matter what.

They Didn't Fight Each Other

They were not jealous of other people's rank or irritated by their actions. They were not worried about the positions of others. They were focused on maintaining their own position. They were not worried about who else had a different rank or a different position, because they were too busy worrying about their own rank, their own job, and their own responsibility to worry about what anybody else was doing. Jealousy and criticism kills.

Our greatest strength is our unity. We are at our strongest point when we walk in unison. We are at our weakest when we allow the erosion of envy and the disruption of disrespect to corrode our unity. We are only as strong as our united front and as weak as our fractured disorder. The theme of novelist Alexandre Dumas (1802-1870), author of *The Three Musketeers,* should be our theme: All for one and one for all.

It would do well for you to pay attention to your place in life and not the others around you. Don't worry about what somebody else is doing. Some people can't do their own job if they're worried about somebody else's job. This just can't be. We all need to focus on our own job, not what somebody else is doing or not doing. When you criticize others, you are not defining them, you are defining yourself. You are exposing your own insecurities and insufficiencies.

If you see that someone has done something wrong, help solve the problem, rather than exposing it. Anybody can criticize; it takes greatness to correct it.

We need to get our focus back. There's a world out there that is so wild and so crazy and so nuts, and it needs Jesus. If we can't demonstrate our love toward each other, how are we going to love the world around us? Don't seek to take somebody else's place, fill your own space. We have enough enemies on the outside trying to bring us down. We don't need to be fighting among ourselves. We need to be totally focused on our real enemies. If we are doing what we are supposed to be doing, we won't have time to belittle the efforts of others.

They Didn't Quit

How are the mighty fallen in the midst of the battle! (2 Samuel 1:25). Lots of people have come up to me and asked me about this person quitting or that person's fall. I admit that it is sad, but I have discovered that for every one who has fallen, there are a hundred that have stood their ground. The media has a phrase that characterizes what they cover in the news: "If it bleeds, it leads." For me, that is a problem. We are focusing on the failures of others when we should be focusing on those who did not give up in the face of unbelievable odds.

I have found that when one person leaves or fails, the person who steps into his place usually does a better job. Isn't that funny? Some of the people I've thought we couldn't do without were replaced by someone who actually did a better job. God always has another one to take their place in the battle. Jonathan and Saul were killed in the battle, but God had a David to take their places. No matter who falls around you, you must not give up.

That's staying in rank; you just keep moving. You don't worry about who's there, who's not there, or who was there. You focus on standing your own ground. You never, never give up. Quitting is a dangerous, demoralizing disease. The great general of World War II, Douglas MacArthur, described quitting this way: *"Age wrinkles the body; quitting wrinkles the soul."*[8]

David was looking for men who would not despair and desert in the heat of the battle—men who would stand their ground. In Revelation 12:11, John described the end-time overcomers with these words, *And they overcame him by the blood of the Lamb, and by the word of their testimony; and they loved not their lives unto the death.* They loved not their lives unto the death. Overcomers do not quit, even in the face of death! As someone has said, winners never quit and quitters never win.

These men were experts at war. They knew how to win a battle. That's why David wanted those kinds of people around him. He wanted certain kinds of people around him who would not abandon him in the midst of the battle.

I know what it takes to succeed in life. I am not oblivious to the challenges. I've done this long enough to know what it takes and what kind of people it will take to make a ministry successful. It takes winners that will not give up at the first sign of conflict and challenges.

I have learned that it is not so much about talent as it is about commitment. It is not so much about ability as it is about reliability. It's about developing principles. It's about advancing in character. It's about consistency and sticking with it. Not everybody can sing and preach, but everybody can be faithful and stand their ground. We need people who will not give up, but who will grow up.

They Were Always There

This final point is similar to not quitting but has a different twist. We need people who will not make excuses for unfaithfulness. I don't look for people who can sing, can play, and can preach. I look for people who know about faithfulness and dependability. I need people who know their place and will stay there in the good times and the bad, in the sunshine and in stormy weather, as well as in times of health and sickness. They make no excuses.

> We need people who have gone through the process and survived to become warriors.

What I expect of others, I demand of myself. I have had to be there when I had hepatitis, when I was shot, when I was betrayed, and when others have left me. Most of us can tolerate a whole lot more than what we think we can. It doesn't take a lot of talent to do that. It takes staying in ranks. It takes staying with it and hanging in there.

David's mighty men didn't change their thinking or their philosophy. They stayed with it. David's men were men of honor and duty, faithfulness and courage, unity and devotion. Winston Churchill described the heart of a warrior with these words, "A man does what he must—in spite of personal consequences, in spite of obstacles and dangers and pressures—and that is the basis of all human morality."[9]

When David needed them, they were there. The world needs a bunch of people who are hungry and desirous of changing the world. We need people who understand the purpose in the process of preparation. We need people who have gone through the process and survived to become warriors. They know how to do battle and are experienced in the war zone.

I pray that God will raise up a new generation of soldiers that will take the battle to the very gates of hell and who will never, no never, give up. We need men and women who know the times in which we live and are committed to staying in rank until the battle is won. God, give us these men and women who know how to fight, can keep rank, and will not go home until the battle is won.

Chapter 12

Preparing for the Future: Build Your Own Altar

"Yesterday is gone. Tomorrow has not yet come. We have only today. Let us begin."[1]

Mahatma Gandhi (1869-1948), preeminent leader of Indian nationalism in British-ruled India, once said that the future depends on what you do today. A victorious future is not a lucky lottery ticket, nor an idealistic fantasy. Your future begins today and is shaped and determined by the actions that you take. Your future success is built upon your present determination and preparation. Building for the future requires a process of planning that begins in the present.

Successful leaders understand this truth: a bright future can only be grounded in the deeds that precede it. The Bible is filled with stories that illustrate how actions today influenced future events. Abraham was willing to leave his own country and travel to a land that he did not know, where he would become the father of nations. Noah built an ark, while others laughed and ridiculed, and he saved a future world. Five wise virgins took extra oil for the marriage festival, and after a night's sleep, had enough when the bridegroom arrived to enjoy the wedding festivities. Solomon spoke of the wise preparations of the ant when he wrote these words. *Go to the ant, thou sluggard; consider her ways, and be wise: Which having no guide, overseer, or ruler, provideth her meat in the summer, and gathereth her food in the harvest* (Proverbs 6:6-8).

Another biblical story that illustrates the value of preparation can be found in the explanation of the ten plagues that had ravaged Egypt. The Pharaoh finally released the children of Israel to pursue their own destiny. After forty long years they began the final march toward their destiny. They marched northward through the Wilderness of Paran and the Wilderness of Zin, doing battle all along the way. At long last, they arrived at the Jordan River, just north of the Dead Sea. They were ready to cross Jordan. They were ready to move in and possess the land that God had given them. They knew that the task of taking the land of Canaan would not be an easy one. There would be opposition, but they were ready.

No One Is Exempt from the Battle

The land on the eastern side of the Jordan River was fertile land, perfect for farming and cattle. Before Israel crossed the Jordan, Moses was presented a request. The tribe of Reuben, the tribe of Gad, and the half tribe of Manasseh said, "This is a nice spot right here. We don't see the point in crossing the river and going over there even though that is the Promised Land on the western side. But this is a good spot right here.

We really like it here. It's fertile land. It is a perfect place for our livestock. Our children can be raised here."

After a time of dialog, Moses agreed to give them that land on one condition. He told them that no one would be exempt from battle. Moses said, "Every man goes to fight." They could not possess that land until they had crossed the Jordan River with their brothers and conquered the enemies in the land of Canaan. If they agreed, Moses would give his blessing.

> The Christian life is not a life that is liberated from conflict and challenges.

Moses' words contain a clear message for all of us. No one is exempt from the battles and troubles of life. The Christian life is not a life that is liberated from conflict and challenges. If someone ever told you that, they were deceived. Retreat is never an option. In order to secure our space in life, battles and struggles will be required.

The leaders of these three tribes agreed to these conditions and would fight with Israel until they had established their place in the lands west of Jordan. So, the men said they would fight. And they did so. They crossed the Jordan and joined their brothers on the other side. Alongside of them, they fought battle after battle until they had secured the land for the other tribes of Israel. Finally, the wars were over and it was time for these two and a half tribes to go back home, to the land promised to them by Moses.

Joshua called the Reubenites, the Gadites and the half tribe of Manasseh and gathered them before him. He commended them for their faithfulness to the promises they'd kept to Moses and let them know that they were free to return to their land. He left them with these final words.

And now the LORD your God hath given rest unto your brethren, as he promised them: therefore now return ye, and get you unto your tents, and unto the land of your possession, which Moses the servant of the LORD gave you on the other side Jordan. But take diligent heed to do the commandment and the law, which Moses the servant of the LORD charged you, to love the LORD your God, and to walk in all his ways, and to keep his commandments, and to cleave unto him, and to serve him with all your heart and with all your soul.

—Joshua 22:4-5

With Joshua's words still ringing in their ears, they crossed the Jordan and settled in on the eastern side. They started getting their families in order, getting their houses built, and began making a life for themselves in the land now known as the Transjordan.

Conflict Threatens the Future

After they got settled, they did something very unusual. It seemed like a great idea but what they did stirred up a hornet's nest. The Bible says they built an altar on their side.

And the children of Reuben and the children of Gad and the half tribe of Manasseh returned, and departed from the children of Israel out of Shiloh, which is in the land of Canaan, to go unto the country of Gilead, to the land of their possession, whereof they were possessed, according to the word of the LORD by the hand of Moses. And when they came unto the borders of Jordan, that are in the land of Canaan, the children of Reuben and the chil-

dren of Gad and the half tribe of Manasseh built there an altar by Jordan, a great altar to see to. And the children of Israel heard say, Behold, the children of Reuben and the children of Gad and the half tribe of Manasseh have built an altar over against the land of Canaan, in the borders of Jordan, at the passage of the children of Israel. And when the children of Israel heard of it, the whole congregation of the children of Israel gathered themselves together at Shiloh, to go up to war against them.

—Joshua 22:9-12

They built an altar on the eastern side. Now, that may not seem like a big deal to you and a casual Bible reader would miss that. What's the big deal? The children of Israel have their altar on the western side of Jordan. Why shouldn't these tribes have an altar on their side of the river?

Well, here is the conflict. There is only one designated altar for the children of Israel and that is the altar in the Tabernacle of Moses. That tabernacle traveled with Israel through the wilderness, across the Jordan and was set up in Gilgal, close to the city of Jericho. After the seven years of war to secure the land, the tabernacle was moved to Shiloh in the hill country of Ephraim, situated almost in the center of the land of Israel at that time. Within that tabernacle was only one altar, the brazen altar, where sacrifices were offered for the sins of the people. You cannot have two or three altars. People did not just build altars wherever they felt like building one. This was almost a heretical thing. It was almost like these people were changing religions. The Law of Moses was clear: only one altar.

When the news of the altar that these tribes had built on the other side of Israel reached the other tribes, they were infuriated. This was a violation of the law and they were prepared to go to war over this disrespect for the Tabernacle of Moses. This action on the part of the two and a half tribes threatened a civil war and could drastically impact the future of Israel. Conflict in life is inevitable. As long as man lives, there will be differences of opinions, disagreements over right and wrong and divergences of plans. Conflict is unavoidable, but resolution of conflict is vital for the world to live in peace.

Conflict Resolution

And the children of Israel sent unto the children of Reuben, and to the children of Gad, and to the half tribe of Manasseh, into the land of Gilead, Phinehas the son of Eleazar the priest, and with him ten princes, of each chief house a prince throughout all the tribes of Israel; and each one was an head of the house of their fathers among the thousands of Israel. And they came unto the children of Reuben, and to the children of Gad, and to the half tribe of Manasseh, unto the land of Gilead, and they spake with them, saying, thus saith the whole congregation of the LORD, What trespass is this that ye have committed against the God of Israel, to turn away this day from following the LORD, in that ye have builded you an altar, that ye might rebel this day against the LORD?"

—Joshua 22:13-16

In an attempt to avoid a full blown war, Phinehas, the high priest and the leaders of the nine and a half tribes, come to their brothers on the other side of the Jordan to confront them. I can hear Phinehas beginning the conversation with these words, "Look, we can't have this. We're not going to have it. You guys are part of us, but look at what you are doing. It looks like you've drifted away from the faith. We will destroy your altar, and we will destroy you if we have to in the process."

Every conflict is filled with negative and positive possibilities. There is the possibility that a conflict can escalate to a point where relationships are broken and lives are destroyed. It takes men and women of courage and wisdom to rise above the conflict and find a way to resolve the issues embedded in the conflict.

The two and a half tribes did not want war. They just wanted to be understood. They wanted the rest of Israel to understand the reasoning behind their action. Here is their explanation.

> *Then the children of Reuben and the children of Gad and the half tribe of Manasseh answered, and said unto the heads of the thousands of Israel, the LORD God of gods, the LORD God of gods, he knoweth, and Israel he shall know; if it be in rebellion, or if in transgression against the LORD, (save us not this day,) that we have built us an altar to turn from following the LORD, or if to offer thereon burnt offering or meat offering, or if to offer peace offerings thereon, let the LORD himself require it; and if we have not rather done it for fear of this thing, saying, In time to come your children might speak unto our children, saying, What have ye to do with the LORD God of Israel? For the LORD hath made Jordan a border between us and you, ye children of Reuben and children of Gad; ye have no part in the LORD: so shall your children make our children cease from fearing the LORD.*
>
> *Therefore we said, Let us now prepare to build us an altar, not for burnt offering, nor for sacrifice: But that it may be a witness between us, and you, and our generations after us, that we might*

do the service of the LORD before him with our burnt offerings, and with our sacrifices, and with our peace offerings; that your children may not say to our children in time to come, Ye have no part in the LORD. Therefore said we, that it shall be, when they should so say to us or to our generations in time to come, that we may say again, Behold the pattern of the altar of the LORD, which our fathers made, not for burnt offerings, nor for sacrifices; but it is a witness between us and you. God forbid that we should rebel against the LORD, and turn this day from following the LORD, to build an altar for burnt offerings, for meat offerings, or for sacrifices, beside the altar of the LORD our God that is before his tabernacle.

—Joshua 22:21-29

In essence they said, "We don't plan to offer sacrifices at this altar. We don't plan on doing any of that. As a matter of fact, we don't really plan on doing a whole lot of anything with this altar. That's done at the Tabernacle. We will still bring our sacrifices there. We are not planning on using this as a substitute."

They continued with these words (my paraphrase), "But, what if we hear that you are not serving God anymore? What if we hear that you aren't serving the God of our fathers anymore? What if we hear that you don't believe the Bible anymore? What if we hear that you, the guardians of the Tabernacle, have forsaken God and are no longer living a holy life, not living a separated life anymore? Do you know why we built this altar?" They concluded their argument with these words, "We built this altar on our side just in case something happens to you folks over there. It is not a substitute for sacrifices. It stands as a testimony, a witness of our commitment to the God of Israel."

The tribes on the eastern side recognized that those on the western side were the guardians of the Tabernacle, and they were not going to interfere with their responsibilities. They just wanted their own altar that would stand if a time would come that those on the western side forsook the God of Israel. That is all that they wanted. This altar would forever be a witness between Israel in the east and Israel in the west that there was no God but Yahweh. This would be a sign between them and the generations to come.

Upon hearing their words, Phinehas and the other tribe members were satisfied and pleased with the response and blessed them. They returned to the other side of the river and reported to their brothers the results of their meeting. All Israel was pleased and war was averted.

Build Your Own Altar

Here is the moral of this chapter: You must build your own altar. Your spirituality and your commitment to Christ cannot be built on the faith of others. Others cannot pray for you the way you can pray for yourself. Others cannot read the Bible for you. Others cannot make sacrifices for you. Only you can build your altar of commitment to Christ. You must pray. You must stand in the time of trouble. You must have your personal walk with Christ. You must trust Him in the difficult times. You must build your life on the principles that are laid out in the Bible.

The tribe of Reuben, the tribe of Gad and the half tribe of Manasseh were saying, "We are not going to use this as a substitute for anything. What if your kids mess up? What if your kids get drawn away by some strange prophet or some strange god or some TV evangelist that's not preaching the truth or living a moral life? We will have our altar that's dedicated to the living God." You must build your own altar.

A few years ago, I was in St. Petersburg, Florida, where I lived as a boy. I went back to the place where my home church was. It was the First Assembly of God church down on 16th Street in St. Petersburg. As I drove into the parking lot, the old building that used to be the church was gone. It had been torn down. An office building stands there now in its place. That's the place where I got saved when I was fourteen years old, and now it is gone!

My thoughts went back to the day that a Christian man picked me up off the street after my mother left me. He paid my way to an Assembly of God youth camp that week. That's where I got saved. When I came back to the church, I lived at the church. My home pastor and his wife took care of me. They basically raised me. I am what I am today because of my home pastor. That pastor and his church were the biggest influences in my life.

Eventually, I became the youth pastor and had youth meetings very similar to what we do here in New York and around the world today. That was back in the 70s. I remember that the room where we had our meetings was totally redone. We removed all the pews, took out the chairs. We painted polka dots on the walls, kind of remnants of the sixties. The kids sat on the floor while we had our youth church.

It was a strange feeling to stand there in that old parking lot looking at an office building where the First Assembly of God church once stood. And as I turned around to get back in the rental car, it hit me. Buildings come and go, don't they? People come and go, don't they? Life can change all around you. People can come and go in your life, but if you have your own altar, you will not be shaken.

You can't live as a parasite, feeding on the spiritual lives of others. I had to learn early in life that I can't depend upon others for my life. I have to learn to stand alone. I have to have my own spiritual experiences with God. I have to build my own faith as I walk through torturous and troubling times. You have to learn to stand on your own. As I have done, you have to learn how to read the Scriptures and let them speak to you. You have to learn how to hear God for yourself.

> Standing alone means you have the strength to stand against the tide of a world going the wrong way.

Don't get me wrong. I believe in going to church. I believe in the necessity of fellowship and friends. But, in the end, you had better know how to stand alone. Standing alone does not mean you are lonely. It means you have the strength to stand against the tide of a world going the wrong way. You have your own testimony of the goodness and the greatness of God that you have experienced in your life.

Building an Altar When Others Fail

I remember the time when I was in Florida and heard that my old Royal Ranger leader slipped away from God and tried to kill his wife because he was on drugs. This guy took us on campouts. He prayed with us. He led dozens of kids to the Lord. He was a big influence in my life. When I heard what he had done, I didn't say anything. Those who know me know that I will never criticize others, but I will pray for them. In that moment of sadness, I turned around while no one was looking, bowed my head and I said, "Thank you, God, I have my own altar." My spirituality and commitment to Christ did not rest on my Royal Ranger leader. I was not crushed by this news, because I had built a life on Christ, the Solid Rock.

Churches pass away. People make mistakes. But, thank God, Jesus Christ is the same yesterday, today and forever. He never changes. He never has, and He never will. Like the old hymn says, "On Christ, the solid rock I stand. All other ground is sinking sand." When you put your faith in anything else, you're going to be disappointed. One of the great lessons I have had to learn is how to survive disappointment. I cannot allow the failures of others to shake me. You cannot build your life on others. They will fail you. I have discovered that you have to transform those disappointments into appointments—appointments with God where you renew your commitments to God and thank Him for the altar you have built.

A few years ago a famous evangelist came to our city to host a one-week television special. I was the featured guest on his show. During that time we hugged each other and he made some pretty special promises to me. He promised that his ministry would help the work we were doing in New York. My expectations ran high, because I thought, *Finally, I can get off the road. This may be the answer we have been looking for. Money will come in to help us pay for more buses and help us to expand our work in the city.* It was not long after hearing those promises that his ministry collapsed because of his moral failure.

Needless to say, the money never came. I know six Assembly of God preachers who have quit the ministry because of what happened with that man. Do you want to know what I did? I went across the street and sat in my office, bowed my head, and said, *"Thank God I've got my own altar."* I am telling you this story to emphasize this truth. Though others fail, you had better have built your own altar so that you will not stumble over the failures of others.

Many promises have been made to me over the years—promises that would help us grow this ministry here in New York. Very few of those promises have ever been fulfilled. Does it hurt? You bet it does. But, I cannot allow my life to be affected by the failures and dishonesty of others. I must move on because I have built an altar.

I have taught our staff and students that they cannot rely upon me for their own spirituality. They have to build their own altar. What would they do if I died in a plane wreck or died from a heart attack? Would their own altar sustain them in a time like that? Nothing will destroy you, if you have your own altar. Though none go with you, will you continue to follow Christ? Is your life built on the life of others, or the life of Christ? Have you built your own altar and will it stand when others abandon or disappoint you?

If You Don't Have It, You are Not Going to Make It

The Jehovah Witness headquarters is located in Brooklyn. When I first moved here I never could figure that out. Brooklyn is not the place for a religious headquarters. Of all the places in America where they could build their headquarters, they chose Brooklyn. Why? I didn't know the answer to that question until a few years ago.

Back in the 1800s, a preacher named Thomas De Witt Talmage (1832-1902) came to New York City. Talmage, who was considered by many to be the "Spurgeon of America," left a dramatic impact on the city. Thousands were attracted by his theatrical style of preaching the Gospel. In those years he was one of the most popular holiness preachers in America.

In 1870, he built his first church, called the Brooklyn Tabernacle in order to accommodate the large crowds who attended his services.

Although the tabernacle could seat several thousand, hundreds were turned away because the church was always filled to capacity. In 1872 his first church building burned to the ground. By 1874 his second church building was built. The auditorium was in a semicircular fashion so that all could see the platform where Talmage preached.

When the second tabernacle was destroyed by fire in 1889, the congregation became convinced there was something fatal about that location. So, they moved to a new location where they built the third tabernacle. In 1894 that church burned to the ground. He had endured much during those days and decided to leave pastoral ministry and become an evangelist.

He turned the church over to another guy who thought pastoring this church was a good deal. Here is the sad part of that story. This guy had been influenced by the Jehovah Witnesses in his earlier days. The man who took De Witt Tallmadge's place, turned the entire church into the Jehovah Witness faith. That church was located right downtown by the Brooklyn Bridge, right where you see the Jehovah Witness office buildings at this time. How did that happen? One man turned the entire congregation.

Do you see how and why that happened? Somebody didn't build their own altar. Somebody was living off of the history and the reputation and the spirituality of Talmage. And when he left, what happened? They were easily seduced by another Gospel, because they had not built their own altar. They were living on the faith of another. Without your own altar, you are not going to make it.

I've seen it for years. Kids go away to youth camp. Everything's nice at camp. It's great. It's wonderful. The problem is that they live in a little religious bubble. And then when they get back home, they lose the spirituality that they gained. I have seen people go away to some great revival or retreat and get all pumped up. The Holy Ghost moved. People speak in tongues. People are set free. They're delivered from sin. But, what happens when they get home? The foundations of their spiritual life had better be more than a temporary experience that moves them emotionally. It must be built upon the Rock of truth and the altar you have built by *your* sacrifices, *your* trust in God, *your* study of the Scriptures, where God speaks to *you* and *you* obey Him.

You must reach the place where nobody, come hell or high water, is going to destroy your faith and your walk with God. Let me say it one more time. If you don't have it, you aren't going to make it. You can't depend on a person or a church. You can't depend on anybody, but Jesus. He's the rock. He told us that on this rock He would build His church and the gates of hell would not prevail against it. You must, personally, build your own altar.

I went to Bible College during the Vietnam War. I saw more kids backslide and lose out with God in Bible College than I have any other place. Do you know why? Because when they were at their home church, they depended on their home pastor. They depended on their mommy and daddy's religion. They depended on the youth pastor's religion and teaching on Sunday morning. When they got to Bible school, all of a sudden, they were on their own for the first time and the weak foundations of their life began to crumble. You had better build an altar that can survive a storm, can survive testing, can survive doubts and can survive other people's failures.

Build Your Altar on the Rock

A few years ago, I was in a place where the pressure of life and ministry was pushing heavy against my soul. I didn't know if I was going to make it or not. The psychiatrist told me to my face, "You're not going to make it, son." After some final words, I got up, turned around and walked out of his office. I'll never forget that day and his words. When I reached the parking lot, I cried out to God, "God, I am going to make it, because I have my own altar, and I'm believing in You." The Christian life is not a PG movie that makes you feel good. You will have your dark moments. You will have times when you are tempted to give up. You will have to face criticism and ridicule. There will be times when you feel alone and betrayed. Here is the truth you must grasp if you are to survive those moments. You have to build your own altar. You have to build your life on The Rock.

One of the ways that Jesus communicated truth was through a story. Jesus was trying to tell His disciples that it is not so much about what you hear as about what you do with what you hear. So, He told them a story.

> *Therefore whosoever heareth these sayings of mine, and doeth them, I will liken him unto a wise man, which built his house upon a rock: And the rain descended, and the floods came, and the winds blew, and beat upon that house; and it fell not: for it was founded upon a rock. And every one that heareth these sayings of mine, and doeth them not, shall be likened unto a foolish man, which built his house upon the sand: And the rain descended, and the floods came, and the winds blew, and beat upon that house; and it fell: and great was the fall of it.*
>
> —Matthew 7:24-27

We have to build our own altar and it is better to build that altar on the Rock. Our faith will be tested and we must not endure those harsh times with resignation, but with burning hope. We have to learn how to transform tragedy into triumph and create our most glorious moments from our hardest trials. No matter what anybody says, no matter what anybody does, no matter what comes my way, I can survive. Why? Because, I haven't built my relationship with God on a man. I haven't built my relationship with God on an organization. I haven't built my relationship with God on a relationship with anyone else. I have built my own altar, and I am firmly fixed on the Rock.

There will be a day when you'll be on the battlefield alone. You have tried to serve God. You have attempted to do the right thing. Instead of applauding you, there will be those that will criticize and spread lies about you. Before I move on, let me say that this is not how the body of Christ is to act. Criticism, gossiping, lying, and jealousy are components of a virus that must be rooted out and destroyed. There's no place for that in the body of Jesus Christ. We're all on the same team here. Let's lift each other up. Let's not drag each other down. Let's hold each other's arms up. Let's pray for each

> When the enemy comes at you like a flood, you have to know that God will raise up a standard against him.

other. Let's brag on each other. Let's pat each other on the back. Don't drag somebody down. If you don't have something nice to say about somebody, keep your mouth shut. Life is hard enough without running the risk of *friendly fire,* and getting wounded by those behind us.

There will come days when dark clouds roll across the sky, when you have decisions to be made. In those moments, you had better be able to seek God on your knees for yourself from your own altar. You had better be able to get down with the blessed Book and read it for yourself and let the Spirit of God speak to you through His holy Word. You had better have your own relationship with God, where you can hear Him clearly. When the enemy comes at you like a flood, you have to know that God will raise up a standard against him. You had better be able to say with faith and confidence, "Bless God. I know my Redeemer lives. I know He lives."

In Luke 18:8 a probing question is asked. *Nevertheless when the Son of man cometh, shall he find faith on the earth?* Will he find a company of men and women who have built their own altar on the Rock of Christ? If you have not built your altar, you'll get discouraged and lose faith. I have seen too many who have given up because they had not built their own altar. They were too dependent on others.

Build your own altar. Make your commitment to not give up in the day of trouble. Be firm in the commitments you have made. If everything else is taken from you—if your heroes die and others abandon you—stand still and know that God is still with you. Remember the altar you built. Remember that living for Jesus is better than living for yourself and others.

Helen Keller once said that though the world is full of suffering, it is also filled with overcoming. The overcomers in this world are those who have built their own altar.

Endnotes

Introduction

1. Marvin Blender, *Never Lick a Moving Blender*, Howard Publishing, West Munroe, LA, © 1996, pg. 45

Chapter One

1. George Eliot, *Wisdom for the Soul,* Gnosophia Publishers, Washington, DC, ©2006, Pg. 401

2. *Eerdmans Dictionary of the Bible,* William Eerdmans Publishing Company, ©2000, Page 227

3. *Critical Thinking Openers Toolkit,* Mark Pennington, Pennington Publishers, Eldorado Hills, CA., © 2010, Page 13

Chapter Two

1. Dr. Shon Neyland, *Devotions from the Desert,* Author House, Bloomington, IN., ©2010, Page 1

2. Andrew Jackson George, *Selected Poems of Robert Browning,* Little, Brown and Company, Boston MA, ©1905, Page 254

3. Wayde Goodall, *Why Great Men Fall,* New Leaf Press, Green Forest, AR, ©2005, Page 111

4. Stephen Pressfield, *Do the Work,* Kindle Edition, Do You Zoom Inc., Irvington, NY, © 2011, Location 85, 86

Chapter Three

1. Henry Ward Beecher as quoted by Laurence Chang, *Wisdom for the Soul,* Gnosophia Publishers, Washington DC, ©2006, page 676

2. Michael Meyerson, *Endowed by Our Creator: The Battle of Religious Freedom,* Yale University Press, United Kingdom, ©2012, page 33

3. Jonathan Edwards, *Sinners in the Hands of an Angry God,* Edited by Wilson Kimnach, Caleb Maskill. Yale University Press, United Kingdom, ©2010, Page 1

4. Ibid, Pg. 1

5. Everett Fox, *The Five Books of Moses,* Shochcken Books, New York, ©1983, Page 443

Chapter Four

1. *The Acceptable Sacrifice,* John Bunyan as quoted in *The Practical Works of John Bunyan,* Hamilton, Adams and Company, London, © 1841, Page 296

2. *The Entire Works of John Bunyan,* edited by H. Stebbing, James S. Virtue, London, © 1859, Page 17

3. *The Treasury of David,* Charles Spurgeon, Hendrickson Publishers, Peabody, MA.,©1990, Page 407

4. As Quoted in *A Life Well Lived,* Charles Swindoll, Thomas Nelson, Nashville, Tn., ©2007, Page 64

Chapter Five

1. Leo Buscaglia as quoted in *EntreLeadership,* Dave Ramsey, Howard Books, New York, ©2011, Page 247

2. Albert Einstein as quoted in *Follow God's Plan and Stop Making Sense,* Lawrence Kinny, Trafford Publishing, Singapore, ©2013, Page 128

3. George M. Halpern, *The Healing Trail,* Basic Health Publications, North Bergin, NJ, © 2003, Page 34

4. Philip Gooden, *Idiomantics,* Bloomsbury Publishing, London, ©2012, Page 251

5. Pat Williams, *Coach Wooden,* Revell, Grand Rapids, MI, ©2011, Page 101

6. Andy Tibbs, *Advertising: Its Business, Culture and Careers,* New York, ©2010, Page 134

Chapter Six

1. Patricia Nuovo, *Soul Accounting,* Self-published ebook, ©2010, Page 64

2. Philip Schaff, *A Select Writings of the Nicene and Post Nicene Fathers,* Christian Literature Company, New York, ©1881, Page 504

Chapter Seven

1. Teddy Roosevelt as quoted by Ronnie Letshabo, *No Limits: A Motivational Guide to Dealing with Challenges,* Quickfox Publishing, Cape Town, South Africa, © 2010, Page 19

2. G. Kleiser, *Dictionary of Proverbs,* S.B. Nangia Publishing, New Delhi, India, ©2005, Page 294

3. Mitch Albom, *The Five People You Meet In Heaven,* Hyperion, New York, © 2007, Page 93

4. Rev. Dr. Horace Williams Jr., *Never Give Up,* Xulon Press, © 2006, Page 29

Chapter Eight

1. Willam Arthur Ward as quoted in *Wisdom for the Soul,* Larry Chang, Gnosophia Publishing, Washington C.C., © 2006, Page 700

2. Renee Brown, *What Are the Temperaments?*, St. Martin's Press, New York City, © 2004, Page 5

3. Watchman Nee, *The Spiritual Man,* Christian Fellowship Publishers, New York, © 1968, Page 247

4. Randall Dickau, *The Road to Begin Your Life,* Author House, Bloomington, Indiana, © 2007, Page 4

5. Eliezer Segal, *Ask Now of the Days of the Past,* University of Calgary Press, Calgary, Alberta, Canada, © 2005, Page 147

6. David Goldsmith, *Paid to Think,* BenBella Books, Dallas, Texas, © 2012, Page 586

Chapter Nine

1. Aldous Huxley as quoted by Diana Whitmore, *Psychosynthesis Counseling in Action,* Sage Publications, London, England, © 2004, Page 13

2. Gina Hens-Piazza, *Abingdon Old Testament Commentaries,* Abingdon Press, Nashville, TN. © 2006, Page 387

3. As quoted by Adam Clarke, *The Holy Bible with a Commentary and Critical Note, V. 1,* published by John Harrod, Baltimore, Md., © 1834, Page 857

4. Randall Roberts, *Lesson in Leadership,* Kregel Publications, Grand Rapids, MI, © 1999, Page 139

5. William Cowper, as quoted by Charles Spurgeon, *The Treasury of David,* Funk and Wagnalls, New York, NY, © 1882, Page 299

Chapter Ten

1. Gaylord Nelson, as quoted by David Young, *Breakthrough Power,* Wind Runner Press, © 2010, Page 147

2. Ronald Reagan, as quoted by Mary E. Ali, *Through Three Miracles,* Dorrance Publishing Company, Pittsburgh, Pa, © 2013, Page 82

3. Alicia Neva Little, *The Story of Marco Polo*, Cambridge Press, New York, © 2010, Page 250

4. Diana Childress, *Marco Polo's Journey to China*, Twenty-First Century Books, Minneapolis, MN, © 2008, Page 53

5. Ken Qualls, *Just Thinking Out Loud*, Self-published book, © 2009, Page 78

6. Ibid, Page 78

7. Alan Armstrong as quoted by Kaneen Morgan, *Finding Your Way*, Author House, ©2013, Page 98

8. Edited by Charles Wallace Jr., *Susanna Wesley: The Complete Writings*, Oxford University Press, New York, ©1997, Page 371

9. John Fletch Hurst, *History of the Church Vol. 2*, Eaton and Mains, New York, © 1900, Page 135

10. Fred M. Barlow, *Profiles in Evangelism*, Sword of the Lord Publishers, Murfreesboro, TN. © 1976, Page 121

Chapter Eleven

1. Brian Klemmer, *The Compassionate Samurai*, Hay House Inc., Carlsbad, Ca. © 2008, Page 1

2. Edited by John M. Muldaer, *Finding God*, Eerdmans Publishing Company, © 2012, Page 3

3. Devin Brown, *The Christian World of the Hobbit*, United Methodist Publishing House, Nashville, Tn., © 2012, Page 127

4. Ibid, Page 128

5. Ibid, Page 128

6. Paulo Coelho, as quoted by Crystal Paine, *Saying Goodbye to Survival Mode*, Nelson Books, © 2014, Page 59

7. Elisabeth Elliot, as quoted by Cheryl Zelenka, *Facing Trials*, WestBow Press, Bloomington, IN. © 2013, Page 25

8. As quoted by Evan H. Offstein, *Stand Your Ground*, Greenwood Publishing, Westport, CN, © 2006, Page 105

9. As quoted by Brett McKay, *Art of Manliness Collection*, HOW Books, Cincinnati, OH, © 2009, Page 234

Chapter Twelve

1. Mother Theresa, as quoted by Garth Johns, *Common Sense Leadership*, Balboa Press, Bloomington, IN, © 2009, Page 145

About the Author

Bill Wilson is the Founder and Senior Pastor of Metro World Child, the world's largest Sunday School, and an international Christian humanitarian organization with headquarters in Brooklyn, New York. Metro reaches more than 100,000 children and their families every week in New York City and around the world. Based on his principle that "it is easier to build boys and girls than to repair men and women," this successful, relationship-centered pattern is currently recognized as one of the top ten influential ministries having the greatest impact around the world today.

Abandoned at 12 years old by his alcoholic mother, Bill's body still bears the scars of several childhood disorders. The painful beginning to his story is the same one he hears from the children he now reaches out to—that they have been abandoned by their families, society and even the agencies who are supposed to care for them. From a timid young boy, he has grown into a messenger of hope in the extreme darkness of today's inner city...and the price for his commitment has been high.

"Pastor Bill," as he is known to the kids, has been hospitalized through the years due to being stabbed, beaten, and shot. Personal adversity has only strengthened his resolve to do "whatever it takes."

Bill Wilson has always believed that what happens *in* you is more important than what happens *to* you.

In 2007, renovations began on the "Metro World Ministries Center." Upon completion, this building will provide facilities to add programs that reach out to the community, as well as Bill Wilson's extensive training program that has proved successful in duplicating his commitment to reach millions of children with the love of Christ.

Pastor Bill speaks at leadership conferences and pastor's schools around the world focusing on reaching families, children, and the cities they live in. His book, ***Whose Child Is This?*** has been translated in 26 languages. The curriculum developed through this ministry is tested and proven in the hardcore, inner-city culture of New York City before being translated into multiple languages and utilized in hundreds of cities worldwide using Bill Wilson's unique concept of "Sidewalk Sunday School."

For more information concerning Metro World Child, please contact:

Metro World Child
P. O. Box 409
Brooklyn, NY 11237
(718) 453-3352

Web site: www.metroworldchild.org

Like us on Facebook at Pastor Bill Wilson

GIVE
an Inner-City
Child
JESUS

Inner cities across the world are full of children who not only need food and clothing, but need to know Jesus. EVERY CHILD should know that he was created with a purpose. Fulfill the Great Commission by joining our Won By One child sponsorship program. Your $28 a month gift will give Metro World Child the tools to provide for a child in New York City or in one of our international locations. You can ensure that their basic needs are met and that he or she has the chance to go to Sunday School.

Serving nearly 100,000 children each week!

METRO
WORLD CHILD
Providing hope. Building futures.

FOR IMMEDIATE SPONSORSHIP CALL
718-453-3352 or visit our website
www.metroworldchild.org

Printed in Great Britain
by Amazon